Get Ready!

FOR STANDARDIZED TESTS

MATH, GRADE FOUR

Other Books in the *Get Ready!* Series:

TEST PREPARATION SERIES

Get Ready!

FOR STANDARDIZED TESTS

MATH, GRADE FOUR

June Heller

Carol Turkington
Series Editor

McGraw-Hill

New York   Chicago   San Francisco
Lisbon   London   Madrid   Mexico City
Milan   New Delhi   San Juan   Seoul
Singapore   Sydney   Toronto

Library of Congress Cataloging-in-Publication Data

Get ready! for standardized tests. Math.
      p. cm.—(Test preparation series)
   Includes bibliographical references.
   Contents: [1] Grade 1 / Sandy McConnell—[2] Grade 2 / Kristin Swanson—
[3] Grade 3 / Susan Osborne—[4] Grade 4 / June Heller
   ISBN 0-07-137399-3 (pbk. : v. 1)—ISBN 0-07-137400-0 (pbk. : v. 2)—ISBN 0-07-137403-5
(pbk. : v. 3)—ISBN 0-07-137404-3 (pbk. : v. 4)
   1. Mathematics—Study and teaching (Elementary)—United States.
2. Mathematics—Study and teaching—Parent participation—United States.   3. Achievement
tests—United States—Study guides.   I. McConnell, Sandy.   II. Test preparation series
(McGraw-Hill Companies)

   QA135.6 .G47   2001
   372.7—dc21   2001030901

McGraw-Hill

A Division of The **McGraw·Hill** Companies

   2 3 4 5 6 7 8 9 0 COU/COU 0 9 8 7 6 5

ISBN 0-07-137404-3

This book was set in New Century Schoolbook by Inkwell Publishing Services.

Printed and bound by Courier.

McGraw-Hill books are available at special quantity discounts to use as premiums
and sales promotions, or for use in corporate training programs. For more information, please write to the Director of Special Sales, McGraw-Hill, Professional
Publishing, Two Penn Plaza, New York, NY 10121-2298. Or contact your local book-
store.

To my fourth grade students, who taught me so much

June Heller

Contents

SKILLS CHECKLIST

MY CHILD ...	HAS LEARNED	IS WORKING ON
ADDITION THROUGH TEENS WITHOUT REGROUPING		
ADDITION WITH REGROUPING		
WORD PROBLEMS		
ESTIMATION		
ROUNDING		
SUBTRACTION		
MULTIPLICATION FACTS THROUGH 12		
MULTIPLYING ONE-DIGIT BY TWO-DIGIT NUMBERS		
MULTIPLYING ONE-DIGIT BY THREE-DIGIT NUMBERS		
MULTIPLYING WITH REGROUPING		
SHORT DIVISION WITHOUT REMAINDERS		
LONG DIVISION WITHOUT REMAINDERS		
SHORT DIVISION WITH REMAINDERS		
LONG DIVISION WITH REMAINDERS		
DIVIDING ONE-DIGIT INTO TWO-DIGIT NUMBERS		
DIVIDING ONE-DIGIT INTO THREE-DIGIT NUMBERS		
FRACTIONS: ADDING SAME DENOMINATORS		
FRACTIONS: ADDING DIFFERENT DENOMINATORS		
FRACTIONS: SUBTRACTING DIFFERENT DENOMINATORS		
EQUIVALENT FRACTIONS		
REDUCING FRACTIONS		
MIXED NUMBERS: ADDING		
MIXED NUMBERS: SUBTRACTING		
PROBABILITY		
DECIMALS		
STANDARD MEASUREMENTS		
METRIC MEASUREMENTS		
IDENTIFY SOLID SHAPES		
IDENTIFY ANGLES		
FIND AREA		
FIND PERIMETER		
IDENTIFY LINE SEGMENTS		

Introduction

Almost all of us have taken standardized tests in school. We spent several days bubbling-in answers, shifting in our seats. No one ever told us why we took the tests or what they would do with the results. We just took them and never heard about them again.

Today many parents aren't aware they are entitled to see their children's permanent records and, at a reasonable cost, to obtain copies of any information not protected by copyright, including testing scores. Late in the school year, most parents receive standardized test results with confusing bar charts and detailed explanations of scores that few people seem to understand.

In response to a series of negative reports on the state of education in this country, Americans have begun to demand that something be done to improve our schools. We have come to expect higher levels of accountability as schools face the competing pressures of rising educational expectations and declining school budgets. High-stakes standardized tests are rapidly becoming the main tool of accountability for students, teachers, and school administrators. If students' test scores don't continually rise, teachers and principals face the potential loss of school funding and, ultimately, their jobs. Summer school and private after-school tutorial program enrollments are swelling with students who have not met score standards or who, everyone agrees, could score higher.

While there is a great deal of controversy about whether it is appropriate for schools to use standardized tests to make major decisions about individual students, it appears likely that standardized tests are here to stay. They will be used to evaluate students, teachers, and the schools; schools are sure to continue to use students' test scores to demonstrate their accountability to the community.

The purposes of this guide are to acquaint you with the types of standardized tests your children may take; to help you understand the test results; and to help you work with your children in skill areas that are measured by standardized tests so they can perform as well as possible.

Types of Standardized Tests

The two major types of group standardized tests are *criterion-referenced tests* and *norm-referenced tests*. Think back to when you learned to tie your shoes. First Mom or Dad showed you how to loosen the laces on your shoe so that you could insert your foot; then they showed you how to tighten the laces—but not too tight. They showed you how to make bows and how to tie a knot. All the steps we just described constitute what is called a *skills hierarchy:* a list of skills from easiest to most difficult that are related to some goal, such as tying a shoelace.

Criterion-referenced tests are designed to determine at what level students are performing on various skills hierarchies. These tests assume that development of skills follows a sequence of steps. For example, if you were teaching shoelace tying, the skills hierarchy might appear this way:

1. Loosen laces.
2. Insert foot.
3. Tighten laces.
4. Make loops with both lace ends.
5. Tie a square knot.

Criterion-referenced tests try to identify how far along the skills hierarchy the student has progressed. There is no comparison against anyone else's score, only against an expected skill level. The main question criterion-referenced tests ask is: "Where is this child in the development of this group of skills?"

Norm-referenced tests, in contrast, are typically constructed to compare children in their abilities as to different skills areas. Although the experts who design test items may be aware of skills hierarchies, they are more concerned with how much of some skill the child has mastered, rather than at what level on the skills hierarchy the child is.

Ideally, the questions on these tests range from very easy items to those that are impossibly difficult. The essential feature of norm-referenced tests is that scores on these measures can be compared to scores of children in similar groups. They answer this question: "How does the child compare with other children of the same age or grade placement in the development of this skill?"

This book provides strategies for increasing your child's scores on both standardized norm-referenced and criterion-referenced tests.

The Major Standardized Tests

Many criterion-referenced tests currently in use are created locally or (at best) on a state level,

and there are far too many of them to go into detail here about specific tests. However, children prepare for them in basically the same way they do for norm-referenced tests.

A very small pool of norm-referenced tests is used throughout the country, consisting primarily of the Big Five:

- California Achievement Tests (CTB/McGraw-Hill)
- Iowa Tests of Basic Skills (Riverside)
- Metropolitan Achievement Test (Harcourt-Brace & Company)
- Stanford Achievement Test (Psychological Corporation)
- TerraNova [formerly Comprehensive Test of Basic Skills] (McGraw-Hill)

These tests use various terms for the academic skills areas they assess, but they generally test several types of reading, language, and mathematics skills, along with social studies and science. They may include additional assessments, such as of study and reference skills.

How States Use Standardized Tests

Despite widespread belief and practice to the contrary, group standardized tests are designed to assess and compare the achievement of groups. They are *not* designed to provide detailed diagnostic assessments of individual students. (For detailed individual assessments, children should be given individual diagnostic tests by properly qualified professionals, including trained guidance counselors, speech and language therapists, and school psychologists.) Here are examples of the types of questions group standardized tests are designed to answer:

- How did the reading achievement of students at Valley Elementary School this year compare with their reading achievement last year?

- How did math scores at Wonderland Middle School compare with those of students at Parkside Middle School this year?

- As a group, how did Hilltop High School students compare with the national averages in the achievement areas tested?

- How did the district's first graders' math scores compare with the district's fifth graders' math scores?

The fact that these tests are designed primarily to test and compare groups doesn't mean that test data on individual students isn't useful. It does mean that when we use these tests to diagnose individual students, we are using them for a purpose for which they were not designed.

Think of group standardized tests as being similar to health fairs at the local mall. Rather than check into your local hospital and spend thousands of dollars on full, individual tests for a wide range of conditions, you can go from station to station and take part in different health screenings. Of course, one would never diagnose heart disease or cancer on the basis of the screening done at the mall. At most, suspicious results on the screening would suggest that you need to visit a doctor for a more complete examination.

In the same way, group standardized tests provide a way of screening the achievement of many students quickly. Although you shouldn't diagnose learning problems solely based on the results of these tests, the results can tell you that you should think about referring a child for a more definitive, individual assessment.

An individual student's group test data should be considered only a point of information. Teachers and school administrators may use standardized test results to support or question hypotheses they have made about students; but these scores must be used alongside other information, such as teacher comments, daily work, homework, class test grades, parent observations, medical needs, and social history.

Valid Uses of Standardized Test Scores

Here are examples of appropriate uses of test scores for individual students:

- Mr. Cone thinks that Samantha, a third grader, is struggling in math. He reviews her file and finds that her first- and second-grade standardized test math scores were very low. Her first- and second-grade teachers recall episodes in which Samantha cried because she couldn't understand certain math concepts, and mention that she was teased by other children, who called her "Dummy." Mr. Cone decides to refer Samantha to the school assistance team to determine whether she should be referred for individual testing for a learning disability related to math.

- The local college wants to set up a tutoring program for elementary school children who are struggling academically. In deciding which youngsters to nominate for the program, the teachers consider the students' averages in different subjects, the degree to which students seem to be struggling, parents' reports, and standardized test scores.

- For the second year in a row, Gene has performed poorly on the latest round of standardized tests. His teachers all agree that Gene seems to have some serious learning problems. They had hoped that Gene was immature for his class and that he would do better this year; but his dismal grades continue. Gene is referred to the school assistance team to determine whether he should be sent to the school psychologist for assessment of a possible learning handicap.

Inappropriate Use of Standardized Test Scores

Here are examples of how schools have sometimes used standardized test results inappropriately:

- Mr. Johnson groups his students into reading groups solely on the basis of their standardized test scores.

- Ms. Henry recommends that Susie be held back a year because she performed poorly on the standardized tests, despite strong grades on daily assignments, homework, and class tests.

- Gerald's teacher refers him for consideration in the district's gifted program, which accepts students using a combination of intelligence test scores, achievement test scores, and teacher recommendations. Gerald's intelligence test scores were very high. Unfortunately, he had a bad cold during the week of the standardized group achievement tests and was taking powerful antihistamines, which made him feel sleepy. As a result, he scored too low on the achievement tests to qualify.

The public has come to demand increasingly high levels of accountability for public schools. We demand that schools test so that we have hard data with which to hold the schools accountable. But too often, politicians and the public place more faith in the test results than is justified. Regardless of whether it's appropriate to do so and regardless of the reasons schools use standardized test results as they do, many schools base crucial programming and eligibility decisions on scores from group standardized tests. It's to your child's advantage, then, to perform as well as possible on these tests.

Two Basic Assumptions

The strategies we present in this book come from two basic assumptions:

1. Most students can raise their standardized test scores.

2. Parents can help their children become stronger in the skills the tests assess.

This book provides the information you need

to learn what skill areas the tests measure, what general skills your child is being taught in a particular grade, how to prepare your child to take the tests, and what to do with the results. In the appendices you will find information to help you decipher test interpretations; a listing of which states currently require what tests; and additional resources to help you help your child to do better in school and to prepare for the tests.

A Word about Coaching

This guide is *not* about coaching your child. When we use the term *coaching* in referring to standardized testing, we mean trying to give someone an unfair advantage, either by revealing beforehand what exact items will be on the test or by teaching "tricks" that will supposedly allow a student to take advantage of some detail in how the tests are constructed.

Some people try to coach students in shrewd test-taking strategies that take advantage of how the tests are supposedly constructed rather than strengthening the students' skills in the areas tested. Over the years, for example, many rumors have been floated about "secret formulas" that test companies use.

This type of coaching emphasizes ways to help students obtain scores they didn't earn—to get something for nothing. Stories have appeared in the press about teachers who have coached their students on specific questions, parents who have tried to obtain advance copies of tests, and students who have written down test questions after taking standardized tests and sold them to others. Because of the importance of test security, test companies and states aggressively prosecute those who attempt to violate test security—and they should do so.

How to Raise Test Scores

Factors that are unrelated to how strong students are but that might artificially lower test scores include anything that prevents students from making scores that accurately describe their actual abilities. Some of those factors are:

- giving the tests in uncomfortably cold or hot rooms;
- allowing outside noises to interfere with test taking; and
- reproducing test booklets in such small print or with such faint ink that students can't read the questions.

Such problems require administrative attention from both the test publishers, who must make sure that they obtain their norms for the tests under the same conditions students face when they take the tests; and school administrators, who must ensure that conditions under which their students take the tests are as close as possible to those specified by the test publishers.

Individual students also face problems that can artificially lower their test scores, and parents can do something about many of these problems. Stomach aches, headaches, sleep deprivation, colds and flu, and emotional upsets due to a recent tragedy are problems that might call for the student to take the tests during make-up sessions. Some students have physical conditions such as muscle-control problems, palsies, or difficulty paying attention that require work over many months or even years before students can obtain accurate test scores on standardized tests. And, of course, some students just don't take the testing seriously or may even intentionally perform poorly. Parents can help their children overcome many of these obstacles to obtaining accurate scores.

Finally, with this book parents are able to help their children raise their scores by:

- increasing their familiarity (and their comfort level) with the types of questions on standardized tests;
- drills and practice exercises to increase their skill in handling the kinds of questions they will meet; and

- providing lots of fun ways for parents to help their children work on the skill areas that will be tested.

Test Questions

The favorite type of question for standardized tests is the multiple-choice question. For example:

1. The first President of the United States was:

    A Abraham Lincoln

    B Martin Luther King, Jr.

    C George Washington

    D Thomas Jefferson

The main advantage of multiple-choice questions is that it is easy to score them quickly and accurately. They lend themselves to optical scanning test forms, on which students fill in bubbles or squares and the forms are scored by machine. Increasingly, companies are moving from paper-based testing to computer-based testing, using multiple-choice questions.

The main disadvantage of multiple-choice questions is that they restrict test items to those that can be put in that form. Many educators and civil rights advocates have noted that the multiple-choice format only reveals a superficial understanding of the subject. It's not possible with multiple-choice questions to test a student's ability to construct a detailed, logical argument on some issue or to explain a detailed process. Although some of the major tests are beginning to incorporate more subjectively scored items, such as short answer or essay questions, the vast majority of test items continue to be in multiple-choice format.

In the past, some people believed there were special formulas or tricks to help test-takers determine which multiple-choice answer was the correct one. There may have been some truth to *some* claims for past tests. Computer analyses of some past tests revealed certain biases in how tests were constructed. For example, the old advice to pick *D* when in doubt appears to have been valid for some past tests. However, test publishers have become so sophisticated in their ability to detect patterns of bias in the formulation of test questions and answers that they now guard against it aggressively.

In Chapter 1, we provide information about general test-taking considerations, with advice on how parents can help students overcome testing obstacles. The rest of the book provides information to help parents help their children strengthen skills in the tested areas.

Joseph Harris, Ph.D.

Test-Taking Basics

At some point during the 12 years that your children spend in school, they'll face a standardized testing situation. Some schools test every year, and some test every other year—but eventually your child will be assessed. How well your child does on such a test can be related to many things—Did he get plenty of rest the night before? Is he anxious in testing situations? Did he get confused when filling in the answer sheets and make a mechanical mistake?

That's why educators emphasize that a child's score on a standardized test shouldn't be used as the sole judge of how that child is learning and developing. Instead, the scores should be evaluated as only one part of the educational picture, together with the child's classroom performance and overall areas of strength and weakness. Your child won't pass or fail a standardized test, but you often can see a general pattern of strengths and weaknesses.

What This Book Can Do

This book is not designed to help your child artificially inflate scores on a standardized test. Instead, it's to help you understand the typical kinds of skills taught in a fourth-grade class and what a typical fourth grader can be expected to know by the end of the year. It also presents lots of activities that you can use at home to work with your child in particular skill areas that may be a bit weak.

Of course, this book should not be used to replace your child's teacher but as a guide to help you work together with the school as a team to help your child succeed. Keep in mind, however, that endless drilling is not the best way to help your child improve. While most children want to do well and please their teachers and parents, they already spend about 7 hours a day in school. Extracurricular activities, homework, music, and play take up more time. Try to use the activities in this book to stimulate and support your children's work at school, not to overwhelm them.

There's certainly nothing wrong with working with your child, but if you're trying to teach the same skill over and over and your child just isn't "getting it," you may be trying to teach something that your child just isn't ready for—or you're doing it in a way that doesn't make sense to him. Remember that not all children learn things at the same rate. What may be typical for one fourth grader is certainly not typical for another. You should use the information presented in this book in conjunction with school work to help develop your child's essential skills in mathematics.

How to Use This Book

There are many different ways to use this book. Some children are quite strong in certain math areas but need a bit of help in other skills. Perhaps your child is a whiz at adding but has more trouble with telling time. Focus your attention on those skills which need some work, and spend more time on those areas.

You'll see in each chapter an introductory explanation of the material in the chapter, followed by a summary of what a typical child in fourth grade should be expected to know about that skill by the end of the year. This is followed by an extensive section featuring interesting, fun, or unusual activities you can do with your child to reinforce the skills presented in the chapter. Most use only inexpensive items found around the home, and many are suitable for car trips, waiting rooms, and restaurants. Next, you'll find an explanation of how typical standardized tests may assess that skill and what your child might expect to see on a typical test.

We've included sample questions at the end of each section that are designed to help familiarize your child with the types of questions found on a typical standardized test. These questions do *not* measure your child's proficiency in any given content area—but if you notice your child is having trouble with a particular question, you can use that information to figure out what skills you need to focus on.

Basic Test-Taking Strategies

Sometimes children score lower on standardized tests because they approach testing in an inefficient way. There are things you can do before the test—and that your child can do during the test—to make sure that he does as well as he can.

There are a few things you might want to remember about standardized tests. One is that they can only ask a limited number of questions dealing with each skill before they run out of paper. On most tests, the total math component is made up of about 60 items and takes about 90 minutes. In some cases, your child may encounter only one exercise evaluating a particular skill. An important practice area that is often overlooked is the *listening* element of the tests and reading the directions, questions, and answer choices carefully. Most of the math questions are done as a group and are read to the

students by the proctor of the test, who is almost always the classroom teacher.

You can practice this by reading the directions to each question to your child. Sometimes the instructions are so brief and to the point that they are almost too simple. In some cases teachers are not permitted to reword or explain, they may only read what is written in the test manual. Read the directions as they have been given on the practice pages, and then have your child explain to you what they mean. Then you'll both be clear about what the tests actually require.

Before the Test

Perhaps the most effective thing you can do to prepare your child for standardized tests is to be patient. Remember that no matter how much pressure you put on your children, they won't learn certain skills until they are physically, mentally, and emotionally ready to do so. You've got to walk a delicate line between challenging and pressuring your children. If you see that your child isn't making progress or is getting frustrated, it may be time to lighten up.

Don't Change the Routine. Many experts offer mistaken advice about how to prepare children for a test, such as recommending that children go to bed early the night before or eat a high-protein breakfast on the morning of the test. It's a better idea not to alter your child's routine at all right before the test. If your child isn't used to going to bed early, then sending him off at 7:30 p.m. the night before a test will only make it harder for him to get to sleep by the normal time. If he is used to eating an orange or a piece of toast for breakfast, forcing him to down a platter of fried eggs and bacon will only make him feel sleepy or uncomfortable.

Neatness. There is an incorrect way to fill in an answer sheet on a standardized test, and if this happens to your child, it can really make a difference on the final results. It pays to give your child some practice filling in answer sheets.

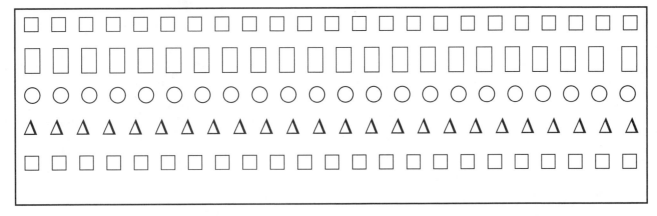

Watch how neatly your child can fill in the bubbles, squares, and rectangles above. If he overlaps the lines, makes a lot of erase marks, or presses the pencil too hard, try having him practice with pages of bubbles. You can easily create sheets of capital O's, squares, and rectangles that your child can practice filling in, or have him color in detailed pictures in coloring books or complete connect-the-dots pages.

During the Test

There are some approaches to standardized testing that have been shown to make some degree of improvement in a score. Discuss the following strategies with your child from time to time.

Bring Extra Pencils. You don't want your child spending valuable testing time jumping up to sharpen a pencil. Send along plenty of extra, well-sharpened pencils, and your child will have more time to work on test questions.

Listen Carefully. You wouldn't believe how many errors kids make by not listening to instructions or not paying attention to demonstrations. Some children mark the wrong form, fill in the bubbles incorrectly, or skip to the wrong section. Others simply forget to put their names on the answer sheets. Many make a mark on the answer sheet without realizing whether they are marking the right bubble.

Read the Entire Question and All the Answer Choices First. Some children get so excited

about the test that they begin filling in bubbles before they finish reading the entire question. The last few words in a question sometimes give the most important clue to the correct answer.

Read Carefully. In their desire to finish first, many children tend to select the first answer that seems right to them without thoroughly reading all the responses and choosing the very best answer. Make sure that your child understands the importance of evaluating all the answers before choosing one.

Mark an Answer before Going On. Many children will sit and worry about a hard question, spending so much time on one problem that they never get to problems they would be able to answer correctly if they only had left enough time. Explain to your child that he can always come back to a knotty question once he finishes the section. Have him mark an answer before going on or put a light pencil mark to be erased later next to the question so that he can go back to it later.

Use Key Words. Have your child look at the questions and try to figure out the parts that are important and those which aren't.

Eliminate Answer Choices. Just as in the wildly successful TV show *Who Wants to Be a Millionaire*, remind your child that it's a good idea to narrow down his choices among multiple-choice options by eliminating answers he knows can't possibly be true.

CHAPTER 2

Addition

The topic of addition does not receive major emphasis in fourth grade because most of the skills have been introduced already in earlier grades. At the fourth-grade level, students will use their addition skills in solving word problems, adding fractions and decimals, calculating measurements, and understanding graphs and data.

What Fourth Graders Should Know

Unless a child has a certified learning disability, it is expected that she will enter fourth grade having memorized basic addition facts through the teens. Your child should have practiced these facts enough so that she can recall them instantly. No finger counting permitted!

Your child also should be able to add two-digit, three-digit, and even larger numbers, both those which don't require regrouping and those which do. (You may know that *regrouping* is also termed *carrying*.) Your child also should be able to add numbers with decimals, placing any decimal point in the correct place in the answer.

Another skill that the fourth-grade child should know is how to add fractions with the same denominators, such as $1/4 + 3/4$. The one new addition concept introduced in fourth grade is how to add fractions with different denominators: $1/4 + 2/3$.

The skill of estimation is one that is really emphasized in today's math classes. Since calculators are used extensively as children learn to solve word problems, it's essential that they be able to quickly estimate if answers are reasonable. In addition, students are taught to "round" two-digit numbers to the nearest tens, three-digit numbers to the nearest hundreds, four-digit numbers to the nearest thousands, and so forth. After the addends are rounded, they are then added for a quick estimation.

Estimation is an area in which fourth graders often need some extra help. For example, a student may be asked to give an estimated answer for the sum of 34 and 58. The addend 34 would be rounded to 30 because the 4 is less than 5, whereas the addend 58 would be rounded to 60 because the 8 is 5 or more. The estimation would be 90. Some text series teach what is called *front-end estimation*. In the problem $34 + 58$, the student is taught to just add 3 and 5 for a quick estimation. Check with your child's teacher or review the math text to see which approach is used.

Students should know the terms *addend* and *sum*. For example, in the problem $3 + 8 = 11$, 3 and 8 are addends, and 11 is the sum.

What You and Your Child Can Do

Practice! If your fourth grader is still counting fingers or doesn't instantly recall basic addition facts, she probably doesn't need to be told how much this is handicapping her math success. It's time for drill and practice! However, don't be surprised if your 9- or 10-year-old resists using flash cards. A trip to your local educational store will yield an array of products for drill and practice that appeal to a child of this age. Self-checking plastic "Wrap-Ups" for practicing facts through 10 appeal to both boys and girls. Various board games are available that provide a fun approach to practice.

Make Your Own Games. For another fun way to practice math facts, buy some spinners and dice to use in simple competitive games you and your child can create. For example, have player 1 spin two times, and add the numbers; then player 2 should spin two times and add the numbers. The player with the larger sum should circle her addition sentence. Play should continue for 10 to 15 rounds; the player with the most circled sentences wins the game. If you need some leverage to keep your child interested, tell her you will play until one of you has won five games.

Math Books. While you're at the educational store, ask a clerk to point you in the direction of the mathematics books. You can find soft-covered books of drill-and-practice problems for all the basic operations using timed practice sheets, usually of 50 to 100 problems. While they are usually not suitable for first- or second-grade students, if your child just hasn't had the motivation to learn her basic facts, these can be motivational and take just a few minutes each day. The exercises are in sequence so that you can easily note progress. Since sheets can't be used more than once, you may want to make copies.

Math Games. If your child needs basic fact practice, check out the math games at the educational store or at your local computer shop. One popular game that seems to attract most kids is "Math Blaster." While you may not see the point of answering basic facts in order to blast creatures out of the air, many kids do find it a painless way to practice their facts.

Estimation Practice. If your child needs practice in estimation, buy two small white boards with erasable markers when you visit the edu-

cational store. When the two of you practice, you write the problem on your board, and ask your child to write the estimate and answer on her board. Fourth graders seem to love using the boards as a change from paper-and-pencil exercises.

Higher Math. Another fun way to have a fourth-grade student practice basic facts is to use the form $(4 + 5) + 9 = 18$. The student first adds the numbers inside the parenthesis and then adds the 9 to that answer. Children at this level seem to be more willing to practice basic facts in this form, perhaps because it appears to be "higher math."

Math in Action. Too many children view math as a dull school subject, with no application beyond math class and the school day. You can help your child enjoy math and provide the motivation necessary to be successful if you show how skills in math are used in our everyday life. While younger children can gain much practical experience through pretending and play, fourth graders are ready for real everyday use of addition. While this may take some *patience* on the part of a parent, between the playful primary years and prealgebra, your creative thinking can provide many practical, hands-on applications of addition skills.

Grocery Store. In addition to having your child keep a running total of your purchases with a calculator, take the time to have your son or daughter compare prices. For example, how much would two of the regular-sized items cost in comparison with one giant size? Is it cheaper to buy the generic item or the top-of-the-line brand with a 50-cent coupon? (This also involves using skills of subtraction and comparison.) The fourth grader who goes along to the grocery store each week will learn quickly the food-buying habits of the family and can be given the job of finding coupons in the newspaper to assist in the shopping. Of course, it can be even more fun if the money saved is a part of the child's allowance!

Keep Tabs… It also would be interesting, and perhaps quite enlightening, to have your child keep records of your monthly grocery bills. The possibilities for application of addition and other math skills in the grocery store are endless but well worth the patience and time it takes on your part.

Restaurant. Buy a small pocket-sized notebook, and have your child record the cost of each item as the family is ordering. While you wait for your meals, your fourth grader should make both an estimate and a true sum of your bill. If a different page is used for each visit to a restaurant and the page is labeled, your child will be able to compare the costs of eating out at various places. If you have a long wait before you're served, the fourth grader also should be taught how to calculate the tip as well as any tax. If there is a special discount for children or senior citizens, all these concepts can be a part of your conversation and teaching while you wait!

Traveling. The possibilities for using addition are endless as the family travels. Again, providing a small notebook (possibly on a clipboard) can help keep your child's work organized and labeled. In addition to keeping a running total of the costs of meals, your fourth grader also can keep gasoline totals and other costs incurred by the family. Calculating miles between cities and total miles traveled for a day are both examples of practical use of addition skills.

Clothing. Having your child keep a record of clothing costs, comparisons among stores, and comparisons of various types of clothing (such as shoes and sneakers) are all ways that she can use addition (and subtraction) skills. Keeping the record also helps to make the child more aware of expenditures and is a valuable time to introduce some ideas about budgeting that are helpful for your family.

Around Your House. If your child is a fourth grader and there are calculations to be done, you should be handing the calculator to your child. Doubling recipes, finding the costs of gardening projects, and calculating the costs of materials for hobbies all should be on your child's list of home responsibilities.

What Tests May Ask

At the fourth-grade level, standardized tests include questions on adding columns of numbers with and without regrouping, adding decimals, adding fractions, and estimating and rounding during addition.

Practice Skill: Addition

Directions: Solve each problem below.

Example:

What is the estimated answer for 51 + 22?

Ⓐ 73

Ⓑ 70

Ⓒ 75

Ⓓ 50

Answer:

Ⓑ 70

---

1 What is the estimated answer for 354 + 543? (Round to nearest hundred.)

Ⓐ 400 + 600 = 1,000

Ⓑ 300 + 500 = 800

Ⓒ 400 + 500 = 900

Ⓓ none of the above

---

2 What is the estimated answer for 528 + 742? (Round to nearest hundred.)

Ⓐ 520 + 740 = 1,260

Ⓑ 500 + 700 = 1,200

Ⓒ 600 + 700 = 1,300

Ⓓ none of the above

3 What is the estimated answer for 45 + 87? (Use front-end estimation.)

Ⓐ 50 + 90 = 140

Ⓑ 40 + 90 = 130

Ⓒ 40 + 80 = 120

Ⓓ none of the above

4 What is the estimated answer for 1,923 + 4,328? (Round to nearest thousand.)

Ⓐ 2,000 + 5,000 = 7,000

Ⓑ 1,000 + 4,000 = 5,000

Ⓒ 2,000 + 4,000 = 6,000

Ⓓ none of the above

5 Solve (4 + 6) + 7.

Ⓐ 9 + 7 = 16

Ⓑ 10 + 7 = 17

Ⓒ 6 + 7 = 13

Ⓓ none of the above

Problem-solving questions are included here to give you an idea of the types of questions your child could answer to apply addition skills.

6 Joe's family traveled 470 miles on Monday, 660 miles on Tuesday, and 576 miles on Wednesday. Calculate both the estimation of the miles traveled and the actual miles traveled.

Ⓐ Estimation is 1,800, and actual is 1,706.

Ⓑ Estimation is 1,500, and actual is 1,706.

Ⓒ Estimation is 1,800, and actual is 1,606.

Ⓓ none of the above

7 At the candy store, an 8-ounce box of chocolates costs $4.49 and a 4-ounce box costs $2.29. If Jane purchases two of the larger boxes and one of the smaller boxes, what is the total cost?

Ⓐ $4.49 + 4.49 + 2.29 = $11.27

Ⓑ $4.49 + 2.29 + 2.29 = about $8.00

Ⓒ $4.49 + 2.29 + 2.29 = $8.98

Ⓓ none of the above

8 Jill kept records on her family's food purchases for a month. Their weekly grocery bills were $50.28, $72.99, $38.24, and $94.72. Her father also stopped several times a week at the local minimarket to buy milk, which costs $2.00 a gallon. If the family used 6 gallons of milk for the month, what was their monthly milk bill? How much did they pay for milk and groceries?

Ⓐ $12.00 for milk, $268.23 for milk and groceries

Ⓑ $2.00 for milk, $256.23 for milk and groceries

Ⓒ $6.00 for milk, $262.23 for milk and groceries

Ⓓ none of the above

(See page 81 for answer key.)

CHAPTER 3

Subtraction

The topic of subtraction does not receive major emphasis in fourth grade because most of the skills have been introduced already in the primary grades. At the fourth-grade level, students will use their subtraction skills in solving word problems, subtracting fractions and decimals, making change, calculating elapsed, or passed, time, and interpreting graphs and data.

Estimation is an important skill in fourth-grade math. For example, a student may be asked to give an estimated answer for the difference of 64 minus 38. The number 64 would be rounded to 60 because the 4 is less than 5, whereas the number 38 would be rounded to 40 because the 8 is 5 or more. The estimation would be 20.

Some text series teach what is called *front-end estimation.* In the problem 64 – 38, the student is taught to just subtract 3 from 6 for a quick estimation. Check with your child's teacher or review the math text to see which approach is used.

What Fourth Graders Should Know

Unless a child has a learning disability, it is expected that the child will enter fourth grade having memorized basic subtraction facts through the teens. Your child should have practiced these facts so that he can recall them instantly without finger counting.

Your child also should be able to subtract two-digit, three-digit, and even larger numbers, including those which require regrouping and those which don't. Your child also should be able to subtract numbers with decimals, placing any decimal point in the correct place for the answer.

Your child also should be able to subtract fractions with the same denominators, such as $3/4 - 1/4$. Subtraction of fractions with unlike denominators is the one new subtraction concept introduced in fourth grade (such as $3/6 - 1/3$).

As we discussed in the last chapter, the skill of estimation in subtraction problems is also emphasized in today's math classes. In subtraction, students are taught to "round" two-digit numbers to the nearest tens, three-digit numbers to the nearest hundreds, four-digit numbers to the nearest thousands, and so forth. Afterwards, the student subtracts the two numbers to find the difference. (Fourth graders also should know the math term *difference,* another word for the answer of a subtraction problem.)

What You and Your Child Can Do

As in addition, it's important that fourth graders see how subtraction is used in their daily lives. Although it does take some time, effort, patience, and creativity on the part of parents, you can provide the type of one-on-one personalized learning that is impossible for teachers to create in school.

Practice. If your fourth grader is still counting fingers or can't instantly recall basic subtraction facts, it's time for drill and practice. Many of the activities and materials suggested in Chapter 2 also would work for practicing the basic subtraction facts. These include soft-covered books of drill-and-practice problems for subtraction.

Although your fourth grader would have been introduced to the concept of regrouping in both the second and third grades, it's not unusual for children to need a review of the concept called *subtraction across 0s* as they reenter school after a summer break. An example:

$$\begin{array}{r} 800 \\ -543 \\ \hline 257 \end{array}$$

Since there are no ones and no tens, the first step would be to regroup the 8 hundreds. Think 8 hundreds = 7 hundreds and 10 tens.

$$\begin{array}{r} {\scriptstyle 7\ 10} \\ 8\!\!\!/0\,0 \\ -543 \\ \hline \end{array}$$

Now think 10 tens = 9 tens and 10 ones. Subtract.

$$\begin{array}{r} {\scriptstyle 7\ 9\,10} \\ 8\!\!\!/0\!\!\!/0\!\!\!/ \\ -543 \\ \hline 257 \end{array}$$

If your child needs practice in estimation for subtraction, consider using the white boards described in Chapter 2.

Calculation Game. Here's a popular game for calculation practice that students enjoy playing in pairs. Begin with a number such as 100. The children take turns subtracting a number from 100, but it must be a number less than 20. The first child to reach 0 is the winner. Depending on the skill level of your child, you can choose different beginning numbers.

Subtraction Cards. Another game that fourth graders enjoy is played with a deck of playing cards (minus the 10s and face cards). Three cards are first drawn from the pile and may be arranged in any order to become the "target number." Each player is then given six cards. These are arranged as two three-digit numbers to be subtracted. Players arrange their six cards so that the difference is as close to the target number as possible. The difference becomes the score for the player; at the end of five rounds, the player with the lowest score is the winner. This game gives children practice with both addition and subtraction calculations.

Parentheses Problems. As we explained in Chapter 2, fourth graders usually enjoy solving problems where parentheses are used. An example: $(10 - 8) + 15 = 17$. Give them some examples; many fourth graders like doing this "grown up" math!

Grocery Store. The most obvious use of subtraction skills in the grocery store would be the use of cents-off coupons and comparison shopping. Your child should use a calculator for this type of problem solving.

Traveling. As suggested in Chapter 2, providing a small notebook for record keeping will be helpful for your child. You might consider putting your child on a "budget" for the vacation, especially if the trip involves stopping at various tourist attractions. Help your child calculate how much he has for souvenirs and snacks for the total trip and for each day. Then he should keep a running total of the amount of money spent and how much is left. If your family calls ahead for reservations, your child also could track the remaining number of miles to your destination. Of course, being aware of cash purchases and the amount of change received is an important math lesson for your child.

Clothing. While it may just seem easier to buy your child what he wants to wear, you can give lessons in lifelong budgeting and money management that are almost impossible for the classroom teacher to provide. Give your child an idea of the amount of money available for clothing. Then, when you are shopping for school clothes, ask him to keep records of what you spend and what is left. This provides practical use of both addition and subtraction skills. Fourth graders are ready for the responsibility of being a part of the purchase decision—and not just from the point of view of what is popular to wear.

Around Your House. If your child is a fourth grader and there are calculations to be done around the house, you should be handing the calculator or pen and paper to the child. Although banking practices are changing rapidly, if you use checks for purchases and keep records in a checkbook, your fourth grader would enjoy doing the subtraction for you. Use of a calculator for these calculations is acceptable.

What Tests May Ask

Standardized tests for fourth graders include questions about subtracting numbers with decimals, subtracting money amounts (in dollars and cents), and multidigit subtraction. There also will be questions on subtracting fractions, which will be written in two ways:

$$\frac{6}{10} - \frac{3}{10} \qquad \text{or} \qquad \begin{array}{r} \frac{6}{10} \\ - \frac{3}{10} \\ \hline \end{array}$$

Practice Skill: Subtraction

Directions: Solve each problem below.

Example:

What is the estimated answer for 522 – 399? (Round to nearest hundred.)

Ⓐ 500 – 300 = 200

Ⓑ 500 – 400 = 100

Ⓒ 525 – 400 = 125

Ⓓ 400 – 300 = 100

Answer:

Ⓑ 500 – 400 = 100

1 What is the estimated answer for 589 – 268? (Round to nearest hundred.)

Ⓐ 500 – 200 = 300

Ⓑ 600 – 200 = 400

Ⓒ 600 – 300 = 900

Ⓓ none of the above

2 What is the estimated answer for 623 – 498? (Round to nearest hundred.)

Ⓐ 600 – 500 = 100

Ⓑ 700 – 500 = 200

Ⓒ 623 – 498 = 125

Ⓓ none of the above

3 What is the estimated answer for 90 – 35? (Use front-end estimation.)

Ⓐ 90 – 40 = 50

Ⓑ 90 – 30 = 60

Ⓒ 90 – 35 = 55

Ⓓ none of the above

4 What is the estimated answer for 5,789 – 2,456? (Round to nearest thousand.)

Ⓐ 5,000 – 2,000 = 3,000

Ⓑ 6,000 – 3,000 = 3,000

Ⓒ 5,789 – 2,456 = 3,333

Ⓓ none of the above

5 Solve (15 – 8) + 12.

Ⓐ 8 + 12 = 20

Ⓑ 7 + 12 = 19

Ⓒ 9 + 12 = 21

Ⓓ none of the above

6 Kara's family traveled 543 miles on Monday and 345 miles on Tuesday. How much farther did the family travel on Monday than on Tuesday?

(A) $543 - 345 = 198$

(B) $345 - 543 = 202$

(C) $500 - 300 = 200$

(D) none of the above

7 At the candy store, an 8-ounce box of chocolates costs $4.49 and a 4-ounce box costs $2.29. If Jane needs 8 ounces, should she purchase the larger box or two smaller boxes? Why?

(A) She should purchase the large box for $4.49.

(B) She should purchase two smaller boxes for $2.29 each.

(C) The costs would be the same, so it doesn't matter.

8 John bought a sweater for $33.99 and a pair of socks for $2.29. If he gave the clerk two $20 bills, how much change did he receive?

(A) $36.28

(B) $3.72

(C) $5.00

(D) none of the above

(See page 81 for answer key.)

CHAPTER 4

Multiplication

Children entering fourth grade have been introduced to the concept of multiplication, in some schools as early as second grade. Teachers have focused on having students understand the concept of multiplication (repeated addition), and students have used various manipulatives as they "discover" what multiplication means. Fourth graders who have this background usually are eager to move into what they see as "higher math."

What Fourth Graders Should Know

An attempt is made to have students memorize the multiplication tables in third grade, although most children seem to need a review as they enter fourth grade. Teachers emphasize the memorization of multiplication facts through 12 so that instant recall is possible. This instant recall makes it easier for children to focus on learning more difficult multiplication procedures, such as multiplying one-digit numbers times two- and three-digit numbers. Knowing the multiplication tables is also the basis for later success in division.

Although most students entering fourth grade have been introduced to the concept that the product of any number and 0 is zero, this concept is reviewed as a part of the multiplication study. When working with flash cards or any practice of the multiplication tables, problems involving 0 are always included.

Children should know the multiplication terms of *factor* and *product*. For example, in the problem $3 \times 8 = 24$, 3 and 8 are factors, and 24 is the product. Fourth graders also should know the terms *skip-counting* and *multiple*. For example, as early as first grade your child should have learned to skip-count by twos, fives, and tens. She can skip-count to find products: 2, 4, 6, 8, 10, 12, 14, and so forth. The multiple of a number such as 5 is the product of 5 and any whole number. The multiples of 5 would be 5, 10, 15, 20, 25, 30, and so on.

What You and Your Child Can Do

In addition to flash cards that you can either make or purchase, there are a variety of fun ways now available for your child to use in learning multiplication facts.

Multiplication Rap. When it comes to multiplication tables, fourth graders enjoy the several different types of "Multiplication Rap" cassettes available. Students enjoy the strong beat to these songs, which are written so that the answer must be given about 10 seconds before it's given on the cassette. These are especially valuable if your child must spend much time in the car traveling to and from music lessons or sports activities.

Multiplication Rock. If your child likes music, the "Schoolhouse Rock" folks also have developed a video called "Multiplication Rock." Its strong beat and catchy songs really appeal to some fourth-grade students.

Board Games. Educational stores also carry a variety of multiplication board games (such as "Multiplication Bingo") that are usually fun for your child.

Speed Drills. You can find books of multiplication facts for speed drills much like what was described in Chapters 2 and 3. This is one activity that usually motivates gifted students, because they can compete against themselves. At most educational stores, you also will find laminated sheets of multiplication facts that have rectangles cut in the space for the answers. These are to be placed over a blank sheet of paper so that they can be used over and over again for practice. These also can be made easily out of 5×8 inch cards.

Spin It! You can use dice or spinners to play multiplication games with your child. For example, pairs of children take turns spinning the spinner two times; the numbers are multiplied together. After each round, the person with the largest product circles her problem. At the conclusion of an agreed-on number of turns, the person with the most circles wins.

Math Out Loud. You can do a number of oral activities to practice the facts, even while driving in the car. For variety, try "The answer is 49, what are the factors?" Or, "The answer is 42, and one of the factors is 6. What is the other factor?" When doing oral activities, do include some reference to odd and even numbers. "The answer is an odd number, and both factors are odd numbers. What are the possible factors." Your child could identify

3×3	$= 9$	5×7	$= 35$
5×5	$= 25$	5×9	$= 45$
7×7	$= 49$	7×9	$= 63$
9×9	$= 81$	9×3	$= 27$
11×11	$= 121$	5×11	$= 55$

It's interesting for children to see that an odd factor times an odd factor gives you an odd number for an answer, whereas an even factor times an odd factor gives you an even number. Of course, two even factors always yield an even number for an answer.

Here, too, the fourth-grade student enjoys the challenge of problems that appear to be more "advanced math." An example would be $(2 \times 9) + (3 \times 1) = 21$.

Play Teacher. Give your child a sheet of multiplication problems you've completed—but include some errors. Tell your child how many errors you made, and supply her with a red pen to circle your mistakes. Correcting the adult is often more fun than doing the problems themselves!

Math in Action. It's interesting for children to "discover" multiplication facts in their environment. Plastic rings around cans of soda come in sets of six. Sets of small windowpanes show multiplication facts. Think of all the things that come in pairs.

Rhyme It. If your child is having trouble memorizing certain facts, have her make up silly rhymes to aid in remembering. An example is

> Eight times eight is sixty-four.
> Shut your mouth,
> And say no more!

Multiplication Party. Another fun activity is to let your child plan a "Multiplication Party." If you're inviting four guests, how many balloons would you need if you have three balloons per guest? Perhaps this could be the reward for your child when she has those multiplication facts memorized!

What Tests May Ask

Fourth-grade standardized tests present multiplication questions in a range of formats, from the very simple (multiplying one digit by two digits) to the fairly complex (multiplying two digits, decimals, and fractions).

Your child also should be prepared not only to select the correct answer from a number of wrong ones but also to realize the possibility that the correct answer may not be listed at all (the classic "none of the above" or "not given" answer choice). This makes guessing much harder.

Practice Skill: Multiplication of Basic Facts

Directions: Solve each problem below.

Example:

$(2 \times 2) + (2 \times 4) =$ ___

Ⓐ 12

Ⓑ 10

Ⓒ 6

Ⓓ 2

Answer:

Ⓐ 12

---

1 $(3 \times 3) + (2 \times 9) =$ ___

Ⓐ $6 + 18 = 24$

Ⓑ $9 + 18 = 27$

Ⓒ $9 + 11 = 20$

Ⓓ none of the above

---

2 $(9 \times 9) - (3 \times 9) =$ ___

Ⓐ $81 - 27 = 54$

Ⓑ $81 + 27 = 108$

Ⓒ $18 + 12 = 30$

Ⓓ none of the above

---

3 $(8 \times 7) - 6 =$ ___

Ⓐ $15 - 6 = 9$

Ⓑ $56 - 6 = 20$

Ⓒ $56 + 6 = 62$

Ⓓ none of the above

---

4 Which equation has the largest product, $(8 \times 8) - (3 \times 3)$ OR $(9 \times 8) + (3 \times 0)$?

Ⓐ $(9 \times 8) + (3 \times 0)$ because the product is 75.

Ⓑ $(8 \times 8) - (3 \times 3)$ because the product is 55.

Ⓒ $(9 \times 8) + (3 \times 0)$ because the product is 72, and this is more than the product of 55.

Ⓓ none of the above

---

5 Julio planned a party and invited five of his friends. He wants to have four balloons for each child at the party and one party hat for each. How many balloons and how many hats must he buy?

Ⓐ 20 balloons and 5 hats

Ⓑ 24 balloons and 6 hats

Ⓒ 4 balloons and 5 hats

Ⓓ none of the above

---

6 One of the games Julio and his friends will play is "Multiplication Bingo." If he wants to have three prizes for each of his friends and he plans to play five rounds, how many prizes will Julio need in all?

Ⓐ He will need 15 prizes.

Ⓑ He will need 18 prizes.

Ⓒ He will need 3 prizes.

Ⓓ none of the above

---

7 Ben and his father are building a fence around their square lawn. They will need nine fence posts for each side of the yard plus a post for each corner. How many fence posts must Ben and his father buy at the lumber yard?

(A) $9 + 4 = 13$

(B) $36 + 1 = 27$

(C) $36 + 4 = 40$

(D) none of the above

8 Brooke and her mother are buying gifts for children at the rescue mission. If there are 12 children at the mission and they want to purchase 4 gifts for each child, how many total gifts must Brooke and her mother buy?

(A) $4 \times 12 = 48$

(B) $12 + 4 = 16$

(C) $12 \times 2 = 24$

(D) none of the above

(See page 81 for answer key.)

Multiplying with Regrouping

Fourth graders who have mastered the basic facts are then moved on to multiplying one-digit numbers times two- and three-digit numbers. This usually has been taught in third grade, but depending on the readiness of the child, multiplying with regrouping may not have been taught. Fourth graders who are finding the multiplication tables challenging, in particular the 6s, 7s, 8s, and 9s, may be introduced to one-digit numbers times two-digit numbers, but the one-digit number will be either 2, 3, 4, or 5. This helps the child feel she is making progress and provides a way to further practice the tables. Don't underestimate the motivational effect of your child being aware of progress and success, even if she's below the class average.

What Fourth Graders Should Know

After students have mastered the basic multiplication facts, they are introduced to the concept of multiplying one-digit by two-digit numbers (such as 7×13). The next step involves using three-digit numbers, such as 2×248. Most basic math books also introduce multiplying greater numbers such as $9 \times 2,889$.

Students who comfortably master these processes usually are introduced to multiplying by tens and ones (for example, 21×17). An additional step that may be introduced is multiplying with three-digit numbers, such as 63×922. Some children enjoy the challenge of multiplying with even greater numbers such as $32 \times 1,205$.

Estimation is again used extensively in multiplying one-digit numbers times two- and three-digit numbers. Your child should be comfortable with estimating products such as 9×456 ($9 \times 500 = 4,500$).

Children should know the multiplication terms of *factor* and *product*. For example, in the problem $3 \times 50 = 150$, 3 and 50 are factors, and 150 is the product.

What You and Your Child Can Do

If your child is having difficulty understanding the process of multiplying one-digit numbers times two- and three-digit numbers, review the procedure:

$$\begin{array}{r} 293 \\ \times 3 \\ \hline \end{array}$$

Think of it this way: $(3 \times 3) + (3 \times 90) + (3 \times 200)$.

1. First multiply the ones. Think 3 ones times 3 ones = 9 ones.

2. Multiply the tens. Think 3×9 tens = 27 tens, and 27 tens = 2 hundreds 7 tens.

Regroup by placing the 2 hundreds above the 2 in the problem.

3. Now multiply the hundreds. Think 3×2 hundreds. Now add all the hundreds: $6 + 2 = 8$.

$$\begin{array}{r} 293 \\ \times 3 \\ \hline 879 \end{array}$$

Teacher, Teacher. Practice to master this concept is essential, but it can become boring to a child, and then mistakes are common. One effective approach that teachers use is to give students 20 problems to complete but tell them to make an error in 10 of the problems. Then have the children exchange papers, give out red pens, and have the "teachers" find the errors. You might try this approach at home. It seems to encourage careful work.

Practice Sheets. You also might prepare practice sheets with parts of the problem completed so that your child can then calculate to find the missing numbers. It's also fun to have pairs (which could be a parent and child) working on white boards. The one working the problem deliberately makes a mistake; if the observer catches the mistake before the problem is completed, that person earns a point. There are many variations on this type of game that the creative parent and child can develop.

Calculator Correct. Another motivational approach is to have a child correct another child's work using a calculator. If a problem's answer is incorrect, the person correcting the paper must find and circle the exact number that is an error and help the owner of the paper correct the error.

Patterns

When teaching two-digit numbers times two-digit numbers, it is usually more effective to have students begin with identifying patterns:

$3 \times 5 = 15$
$30 \times 5 = 150$
$30 \times 50 = 1,500$
$30 \times 500 = 15,000$
$30 \times 5,000 = 150,000$

Fourth-grade students should realize that when there are zeroes in either of the factors, the number of zeros in the product is equivalent to the number of zeroes in the factors. However, 4×5, 5×6, and 8×5 should receive some special emphasis. For example, in 40×500, it should be emphasized that students first multiply $4 \times 5 = 20$. Then the additional zeroes should be added to get 20,000.

Understanding this concept of counting zeroes is also valuable when students are estimating products. For example, in the problem 24×556:

1. Round 24 to 20 and 556 to 600.

2. Then think $2 \times 6 = 12$.

3. Add the zeroes from the rounded factors to the 12 to get 12,000.

Your child should know that this is estimation by rounding.

If your child seems confused by two-digit times two-digit multiplication, take her through the process step by step. For example:

$$\begin{array}{r} 85 \\ \times 24 \\ \hline \end{array}$$

It is usually effective to have your child cover the numeral in the tens place (2) and multiply the 4 ones times 85. It makes the new process seem easier if your child realizes that she already knows what to do for the first line in the answer.

$$\begin{array}{r} 2 \\ 85 \\ \times 24 \\ \hline 340 \end{array}$$

Note that there is regrouping when your child multiplies 4 ones times 5 ones. If the child places a 2 above the 8, when that is added to $4 \times 8 = 32$, have your child draw a line through the 2. At times this can be confusing to the students as they begin to multiply the tens for the second line.

$$\begin{array}{r} \cancel{2} \\ 85 \\ \times 24 \\ \hline 340 \\ 0 \end{array}$$

Now have your child place a zero under the 0 in the first line. Explain that the child is multiplying by tens for the second row and not by ones; this is the reason that a 0 always should be placed in the ones column for the second row. This is often called a *place holder* in basic texts. It is an important concept to stress so that students do not place the tens product in the ones column.

$$\begin{array}{r} 1\cancel{2} \\ 85 \\ \times 24 \\ \hline 340 \\ 1700 \end{array}$$

Think 2×5 is 10, with the 1 to be regrouped and placed above the 8. Then think 2×8 is 16, and add the 1 to be regrouped to have 17 hundreds.

$$\begin{array}{r} 1\cancel{2} \\ 85 \\ \times 24 \\ \hline 340 \\ 1700 \\ \hline 2040 \end{array}$$

Now the products are added.

Here, too, practicing these types of problems for long periods of time can lead to careless mistakes. It is more effective to have children locate errors or add missing numbers or correct the work of other children. You and your child can use some creative approaches at home if she needs some additional practice.

If your child's class is doing double-digit multiplication and she is still struggling with the basic facts, use problems with easier multiplication products so that she will understand the process and feel successful. You can challenge your fourth grader with more complicated problems once she is more comfortable with the 7s, 8s, and 9s tables. Remember that the challenging process of two-digit numbers times two-digit numbers is a "big deal" for fourth graders, almost like a rite of passage. Just use easier factors for the child who is still struggling with the tables.

Practice Skill: Multiplying with Regrouping

Directions: Multiply. Don't forget to use commas.

Example:

$2,000 \times 6 =$ ___

Ⓐ 120,000

Ⓑ 12,000

Ⓒ 2,000

Ⓓ 6,000

Answer:

Ⓑ 12,000

9 $3,000 \times 6 =$ ___

Ⓐ 6,000

Ⓑ 3,000

Ⓒ 18,000

Ⓓ 20,000

10 $60 \times 90 =$ ___

    Ⓐ 9,000

    Ⓑ 6,000

    Ⓒ 5,400

    Ⓓ 54,000

11 $400 \times 60 =$ ___

    Ⓐ 24,000

    Ⓑ 2,400

    Ⓒ 6,400

    Ⓓ 64,000

12 $500 \times 60 =$ ___

    Ⓐ 50,000

    Ⓑ 60,500

    Ⓒ 30,000

    Ⓓ 300,000

13 $50 \times 80 =$ ___

    Ⓐ 800

    Ⓑ 8,500

    Ⓒ 4,000

    Ⓓ 40,000

14 $400 \times 5 =$ ___

    Ⓐ 20,000

    Ⓑ 2,000

    Ⓒ 200,000

    Ⓓ 5,400

Directions: Multiply and find the correct answer.

Example:

$$\begin{array}{r} 38 \\ \times 32 \\ \hline \end{array}$$

    Ⓐ 1,216

    Ⓑ 160

    Ⓒ 2,984

    Ⓓ 2,216

Answer:

    Ⓐ 1,216

15
$$\begin{array}{r} 29 \\ \times 43 \\ \hline \end{array}$$

    Ⓐ 1,204

    Ⓑ 1,247

    Ⓒ 1,188

    Ⓓ 1,089

16
$$\begin{array}{r} 14 \\ \times 43 \\ \hline \end{array}$$

    Ⓐ 559

    Ⓑ 588

    Ⓒ 602

    Ⓓ 492

17
$$\begin{array}{r} 23 \\ \times 44 \\ \hline \end{array}$$

    Ⓐ 1,012

    Ⓑ 902

    Ⓒ 968

    Ⓓ 989

18   13
      $\times 23$

(A) 286

(B) 299

(C) 264

(D) 289

(See page 81 for answer key.)

CHAPTER 5

Division

Children entering fourth grade already have been introduced to the concept of division. Many times this was first introduced informally into the curriculum by dividing snacks or school supplies. Teachers in the primary grades also have focused on having students understand the concept of division through using various manipulatives. Fourth graders who have this background usually are eager to move into what they see as "higher math."

What Fourth Graders Should Know

An attempt is made to have students memorize basic division facts in third grade, although most children seem to need a review as they enter fourth grade. Teachers will have students memorize basic division facts through 12 so that instant recall is possible. This instant recall makes it easier for children to focus on learning more difficult division processes.

An additional concept that is revisited here is *fact families*. Students have used the term in first and second grades as they learned about addition and subtraction. For example, the fact family for 2, 5, and 7 is

$$2 + 5 = 7 \qquad 7 - 5 = 2$$
$$5 + 2 = 7 \qquad 7 - 2 = 5$$

In fourth grade, students learn the inverse relationship between multiplication and division when they write the fact family for 3, 7, and 21 (an example):

$$3 \times 7 = 21 \qquad 21 \div 7 = 3$$
$$7 \times 3 = 21 \qquad 21 \div 3 = 7$$

Children should know the terms *divisor, dividend,* and *quotient.* For example, in the problem $60 \div 6 = 10$, 6 is the divisor, 60 is the dividend, and 10 is the quotient. Students entering fourth grade also have been introduced to the three forms for writing division signs.

What You and Your Child Can Do

Missing Factor. Spend some time playing missing factor types of games with your child. For example, give your child the sentence $3 \times \underline{\quad} = 12$, and read it: "Three times what number equals 12." The child should answer "4." Then show your child the related division fact; "12 divided by 3 equals 4."

Fact Families. Guide your child through writing different fact families. Given 3, 4, and 12, expect him to write the four facts: $3 \times 4 = 12$, $4 \times 3 = 12$, $12 \div 4 = 3$, and $12 \div 3 = 4$.

Counter Culture. If your child seems confused about finding missing factors, spend several short sessions having him use counters (cereal, buttons, and so on). For example, count out 18 buttons. Make six sets, with an equal number of buttons in each set. How many sets have you made? Then ask your child if he can divide the 18 buttons into equal sets any other way ($18 \div 2$, $18 \div 3$). Make sure that he writes the division fact after showing you the way the 18 buttons are divided.

Board Games. A stop at the local educational store also will yield a number of board games such as Division Bingo. One bingo type of game is called *Quizo* (Materials Media), in which the cards have multiplication products on one side and division quotients on the other. You also can buy division "wrap-ups" and "division rap" cassettes that emphasize the basic division facts.

As your child practices the basic division facts, revisit some of the approaches suggested in earlier chapters, such as providing problems with parentheses:

$$(12 \div 6) + 25 = 27$$

Young Musicians. If your child takes any type of music lesson or shows an interest in music, you can link music to division. For example, review the fact that two half notes are the same as one whole note. Then ask such questions as: "How many whole notes make the same time value as 6 half notes?" $(6 \div 2 = 3)$

Children have been introduced to the concept "zero divided by any number is zero." You should include a review of this concept as you work with your fourth-grade child. If you're using flash cards or giving your child basic fact division problems on a white board, make sure you include some $0 \div 7$ types of problems.

What Tests May Ask

Standardized tests in fourth grade present questions in both short and long division with and without remainders using all division symbols. Students will be asked to choose the correct answer from a group of possibilities, sometimes including "none of the above" or "not given."

Two- and Three-Digit Numbers

Fourth graders who have mastered the basic facts are then moved on to dividing one-digit numbers into two- and three-digit numbers. They should be comfortable with division with-

out remainders before being introduced to division with remainders.

Fourth graders who find the basic division facts to be challenging (especially the 6s, 7s, 8s, and 9s) may be introduced to one-digit divisors with two- and three-digit divisors, but the one-digit divisors will be either 2, 3, 4, or 5. This helps the child feel that he is making progress, and provides a way to further practice basic division facts. Don't underestimate the motivational effect of your child being aware of progress and success, even if the student is below the class average.

What Fourth Graders Should Know

After fourth-grade students have mastered the basic division facts, they are introduced to the concept of dividing two- and three-digit numbers by a one-digit number with remainders. For example:

$$729 \div 8 = 81, r\ 8$$

Students who comfortably master this process usually are introduced to problems involving division by multiples of 10. An additional skill introduced to some fourth-grade students is dividing three- and four-digit numbers by two-digit numbers. Most parents know this procedure as *long division*.

However, the emphasis in fourth grade is on using multiples of 10 as the two-digit number for long division. Students who become very comfortable with this skill in fourth grade usually do a fine job with more complicated numbers in fifth grade. A fourth grader should be quite comfortable with using multiples of 10 before he is challenged with more complicated two-digit divisors such as 79, 23, or 58.

Children should know the terms *divisor, dividend,* and *quotient.* For example, in $60 \div 6 = 10$, 6 is the divisor, 60 is the dividend, and 10 is the quotient.

Your child also should be familiar with the term *remainder.* When there is no remainder, students say that the dividend is *divisible* by the divisor. This is a term your fourth-grade child should be able to use correctly.

What You and Your Child Can Do

Using paper and pencil or a white board, give your child plenty of practice doing rather simple division problems with remainders. While your child is practicing, and before moving onto long division forms, it is generally a good time to look at division patterns involving zeroes. Examples of this type of problem would be

$$9 \div 9 = 1$$
$$90 \div 9 = 10$$
$$900 \div 9 = 100$$
$$9,000 \div 9 = 1,000$$

Make sure that your child solves the basic division fact before counting the zeroes to complete the problem. Refer back to the multiplication patterns that your child has already mastered.

It is usually easier for students to be introduced to this form of long division when they are dividing three- or four-digit numbers by one-digit numbers. Use easy division facts until your child is comfortable with the process.

Remember that always requiring a child to check answers can be tiring. Vary the procedure by permitting him to sometimes use a calculator for checking.

Memory Trick. Notice that the procedure for long division involves the steps of divide, multiply, subtract, compare, and bring down. It is sometimes easier for some students to remember the process if it is presented in terms of a family: *d*ad, *m*other, *s*ister, *c*ousins, and *b*rother. A memory aid like this does seem to help some children remember the procedure.

Pairs. In this game, each player needs two sets of cards numbered 1 to 9.

1. Mix the number cards in one pile.
2. Each player draws four cards.

3. Players use their cards to each make a three-digit dividend and a one-digit divisor.
4. The goal of the game for each round is to arrange the cards to make the largest possible quotient. You can vary the game by calling for the smallest possible quotient. The player who wins the round gets a point. Then shuffle the cards, and start the next round. At the end of an agreed on number of rounds, the player with the most points is the winner. You could create the same type of game using a spinner or dice.

Estimate! If you find that your child is having trouble estimating the first digit of the quotient, try a series of estimation problems. This always seems to give students extra confidence. Give your child a problem such as $478 \div 9$ in the form $9\overline{)478}$. Notice that the hundreds digit is less than 9, so have your child underline the 47. Have him determine that the fact 9×5 is nearly 47, and then add a 0 because there is one more digit. This approach isn't necessary for all students but is always helpful if a child is having difficulty estimating the first number in the quotient. After your child is comfortable with the long division form using one-digit divisors, move on to quotients containing zeroes.

Practice Skill: Division

Directions: Complete each problem.

Example:

$525 \div 5 = \_\_\_$
- Ⓐ 105
- Ⓑ 5
- Ⓒ 25
- Ⓓ 20

Answer:
- Ⓐ 105

1 $538 \div 3 =$ ___

   Ⓐ 178, r 3

   Ⓑ 179, r 1

   Ⓒ 178

   Ⓓ not given

2 $30 \div 6 =$ ___

   Ⓐ 6

   Ⓑ 7

   Ⓒ 5

   Ⓓ not given

3 $20 \div$ ___ $= 10$

   Ⓐ 5

   Ⓑ 4

   Ⓒ 2

   Ⓓ not given

4 $45 \div$ ___ $= 9$

   Ⓐ 8

   Ⓑ 6

   Ⓒ 2

   Ⓓ 5

Directions: Read the following problems, and choose the correct answer. Remember to calculate the quotient inside the parentheses before adding or subtracting another number.

Example:

   $(12 \div 2) + 2 =$ ___

   Ⓐ 6

   Ⓑ 8

   Ⓒ 12

   Ⓓ 1

Answer:

   Ⓑ 8

5 $(20 \div 2) + 5 =$ ___

   Ⓐ 10

   Ⓑ 5

   Ⓒ 15

   Ⓓ none of the above

6 $(6 \div 2) + 2 =$ ___

   Ⓐ 5

   Ⓑ 6

   Ⓒ 12

   Ⓓ 20

(See page 81 for answer key.)

CHAPTER 6

Fractions and Probability

The study of fractions and probability just doesn't get enough emphasis in some elementary schools. Concepts related to understanding fractions and probability should be taught with many opportunities for hands-on activities, such as cooking, measuring, and playing games of chance. Students need time to fold and divide paper squares, circles, and rectangles into halves, thirds, fourths, and so forth. Elementary school children also need the time to use manipulatives to find and understand equivalent fractions. Without a background of being able to discover and explore in the primary grades, fourth-grade students can find the study of fractions to be quite challenging.

With luck, your child's third-grade teacher has had some time to introduce the topic of probability. However, skills related to probability don't usually receive major emphasis at any grade level in elementary schools. This is usually due to a lack of time.

What Fourth Graders Should Know

Students entering fourth grade are expected to know how to identify and label fractional parts of a figure, as well as parts of a group. Even though students have been introduced to the concept of finding a part of a group, such as $\frac{1}{3}$ of 12 or $\frac{1}{4}$ of 16, this is usually reviewed before students move on to solving more difficult problems. Examples would be $\frac{2}{3}$ of 15 or $\frac{3}{4}$ of 20.

In third grade, students have been introduced to the term *equivalent fractions* and usually show a good understanding if much of their work has been done with manipulatives. Fourth-grade students are taught to multiply or divide the numerator and the denominator by the same number in order to find the equivalent fractions. Students also are expected to compare and order fractions.

The concept of adding and subtracting fractions with like denominators should be reviewed before students are introduced to these operations when problems have unlike denominators. Adding and subtracting *mixed numbers* (which are whole numbers and a fraction, such as $1\frac{1}{2}$) is also incorporated into any fractional unit in fourth grade. Students who have easily mastered these concepts may be taught to multiply fractions, a concept that is usually introduced in fifth grade.

Children entering fourth grade should know the terms *fraction, numerator* and *denominator*. A *fraction* is a number that names part of a group or part of a whole. Here's a good way to help your child remember the terms: In a fractional number, the ***D**enominator* is "**D**own below the line," and the *Numerator* is "**N**ot." Fourth graders review the meaning of *equivalent fractions,* which are fractions that name the same number. They also will review the meaning of the terms *improper fraction* (an example is $\frac{9}{4}$) and *mixed number,* which is a whole number and a fraction. Other terms that receive major emphasis in fourth grade are *simplifying frac-*

tions and *common factors*. These will be explained under the "What You and Your Child Can Do" section of this chapter.

Most third graders are introduced to simple probability experiments. For example, if you toss a coin 50 times, will there be more heads or more tails? In fourth grade, your child will be exposed to experiments that are more challenging. Students should define *probability* as the chance that something may happen.

What You and Your Child Can Do

Review. As the topic of fractions is introduced in fourth grade, teachers often have students review by folding and cutting squares, circles, or rectangles into halves, thirds, fourths, eighths, sixteenths, and so forth. You can give your child a chance to further explore these concepts by providing supplies for exploring fractions at home.

Manipulatives. In addition to folding and cutting paper into fractional parts, provide your child with beads, cereal, candy, or other manipulatives so that she also can practice finding a fractional part of a group. Of course, something edible is always more fun! For example: given 10 M&M's, with 8 blue and 2 yellow ones, most children at this level can easily tell you that 2 out of 10 ($2/10$) are yellow and that 8 out of 10 ($8/10$) are blue.

However, they are more challenged when asked to tell $2/3$ of 12. Although this concept most likely will have been introduced in third grade, review with your child before introducing problems with a numerator of more than one. Count out 12 pieces of cereal. Look at the denominator, and divide the 12 pieces of cereal into 3 groups. There are 4 pieces in each group. Then check the numerator, which is a 2. This means that the child should count the number of pieces in 2 of her groups. The answer is 8. Your child should be encouraged to use manipulatives to help find a fraction of a number.

Word Find. Students at this level usually enjoy finding words that show fractions. For example,

find a word where the vowels are $1/4$ of the letters. Find a word where $2/4$ of the letters are *t*'s.

Pattern Blocks. Teachers sometimes will use pattern blocks to help students identify and read fractions for parts of regions. These blocks are available at most educational stores and are an excellent way to have your child build background for an understanding of equivalent fractions. Soft-cover booklets also are available that contain templates and suggestions for exploring fractions through the use of pattern blocks. These are quite easy to use.

Fraction Bars. Fraction bars are very useful in helping children identify equivalent fractions. These are available commercially, although it is also easy to make a set out of cardboard or heavy construction paper. Make them all on the same paper for easy reference.

1. Begin with a strip 12 inches long and about $1\frac{1}{2}$ inches wide.
2. Label this one whole, or $1/1$.
3. Cut seven additional strips, also 12 inches long.
4. Fold and divide one strip into halves, another into fourths, another into eighths, and another into twelfths.
5. Add fifths, thirds, sixths, tenths, and so forth for additional exploration.

Using the fraction bars, it's easy for your child to see, for example, that $1/4$ and $1/4$ is the same as $1/2$ or that $2/10$ is the same as $1/5$. You also might have your child begin with a circle, cut a number of equal circles, and then prepare a set of fraction circles. Children also can see equivalent fractions on a ruler.

Have the fraction bars available for reference when you ask your child to compare fractions, such as arranging a set of fractions from least to greatest. Always begin by having your child compare just two fractions before moving on to giving her three or more fractions to place in order. Make sure that your child notices that equivalent fractions with the same denominator are compared by looking at the numerator. When your child is not using fraction bars to compare fractions, then she should find the common denominator for the fractions before comparing their values. For example, if you ask your child to compare ¾, ⅓, and ⅚, these should be changed to the common denominator of 12 before the comparison is made.

$$\frac{3}{4} = \frac{9}{12} \qquad \frac{1}{3} = \frac{4}{12} \qquad \frac{5}{6} = \frac{10}{12}$$

Finding the common denominator makes the comparison easy for a child to make.

In the classroom, students usually are given time to work with manipulatives, such as fraction bars, before being taught to find equivalent fractions by multiplying.

To find an equivalent fraction for ⅔, multiply both the numerator and denominator by the same number:

$$\frac{2 \times 2 = 4}{2 \times 3 = 6}$$

An equivalent fraction for ⅔ is 4/6. Have your child check her answer using fraction bars. In addition, students at this level should know that dividing is another way to identify equivalent fractions. To find the equivalent fraction for 4/16, divide both the numerator and the denominator by 4. Again, make sure that this paper and pencil work is checked with the fraction bars. Fourth graders usually have fun writing equivalent fraction clues. Here's an example:

The denominator of this fraction is 4.
An equivalent fraction is 8/16.
What is the fraction?

While third graders have many experiences with finding equivalent fractions, the topic of simplifying fractions is usually a new one to fourth graders. A fraction is in its simplest form when the numerator and the denominator have no factors common to both that are greater than 1.

Simplify 2/10 by dividing the numerator and denominator by the largest common factor.

Factors of 2:   2
Factors of 10:   2, 5
Common factors: 2

Now divide the numerator and the denominator by 2. When learning to simplify fractions, it is generally quite helpful to have a student write out the factors for both the numerator and the denominator of the fraction and circle the greatest common factor before dividing. Lots of practice with listing factors gives students a clear picture of the concept *greatest common factor*.

Most students have been introduced to the terms *improper fraction* and *mixed number* before entering fourth grade. The numerator of an improper fraction is equal to or greater than the denominator: 9/5 is an improper fraction. Renaming an improper fraction to a mixed number is a paper and pencil skill that takes some practice. To rename 9/5:

1. Divide the numerator by the denominator: 9 divided by 5 is 1, with a remainder of 4.

2. Write the quotient (1) as the whole-number part; write the remainder (4/5) over the divisor as the fraction part.

3. Students should be reminded to make sure that the fraction part of the mixed number is in its simplest form.

Fourth-grade students generally have done some adding and subtracting of fractions with like denominators in third grade. However, it is always helpful to review this procedure before moving on to the more challenging processes of adding and subtracting with unlike denominators.

If your child seems to lack confidence when learning more challenging concepts, give her lots of experience with naming common denominators before working with addition and subtraction of fractions. For example, what is a common denominator of ½ and 3/7 (14), and what is a common denominator of $6/7$ and $4/14$ (14)?

Fraction Index Cards. You can avoid having to constantly make new problems every time you want to have your child practice adding and subtracting if you write fractions on 3×5 inch index cards. When you want your child to do 10 minutes of practice, have her shuffle the cards and place them face down. Draw two cards to use to make the problems. Of course, this means that your child must know enough about comparing fractions to place the larger of the two fractions as the number to be subtracted from.

Mixed Numbers

One additional fraction concept taught in fourth grade is the addition and subtraction of mixed numbers. If you're reviewing this concept with your child, begin by having her add mixed numbers with like denominators. This will give your child a chance to become familiar with the process of simplifying a mixed-number answer before also having to deal with unlike denominators.

At this level, the most challenging types of problems are those with answers such as $2^{11}/_9$, where the child is expected to take the improper fraction of $^{11}/_9$ and make it into the mixed number $1^2/_9$ and add this to the 2 ($1^2/_9 + 2 = 3^2/_9$). Another example would be an answer of $4^5/_5$; the fraction of $^5/_5$ is equal to 1 ($1 + 4 = 5$). This type of problem isn't emphasized in textbooks yet does appear occasionally on achievement and other types of math tests.

If your child finds the topic of fractions to be challenging, do check out what is available at your local educational store. Learning Resources makes a set of 100 Fraction Circle Flash Cards that contains 100 flash cards and 5 cards with suggested activities. One side of each card shows a picture of a shaded region of a circle; the other side shows the fractional numeral with its fraction name. You will find other helpful games and activities that your child will enjoy using at home.

Probability Spinners. While you're at the educational store, check for some "probability spinners," which you and your child can use for playing games. For example, suppose you use a spinner divided into four equal regions, colored red, blue, green, and yellow. If your child scores a point each time the spinner lands on yellow, and you score a point when the spinner lands on red, blue, or green, who has the highest probability of winning the most points? Spinners with unequal fractional parts colored give you the opportunity to discuss other probabilities or "possible outcomes."

You also might illustrate probabilities by putting M&M's in a paper bag. For example, use 10 green, 10 yellow, 4 red, and 1 brown. Discuss the probability of picking brown and yellow, or red and green, or yellow and green. Then have your child chart what color is picked each time she reaches into the bag (not looking, of course). Is the probability different if the M&M's are returned to the bag after each recording versus not returning the chosen pieces to the bag?

Students at this level also are introduced to the terms *number of favorable outcomes* and *number of possible outcomes*. For example, suppose that you are playing a game with two dice. You will gain a point if you roll a 1 or 2.

Your *number of favorable outcomes* is 2 (1 or 2).
Your *number of possible outcomes* is 6 (1, 2, 3, 4, 5, 6).
The *probability* of you winning is $2/_6$.

Use coins (heads and tails), different colored cubes, numbers on cards, and other manipulatives as you practice this skill with your child. Help your child to further understand the concept of probability by calling attention to its use in daily life.

What Tests May Ask

As a way of testing the extent to which your fourth grader has understood math concepts, many types of standardized tests will measure how well your child can order fractions from smallest to largest and add, subtract, and reduce fractions and determine simple probability. They may ask for fractions' other names (as in "What's another name for ³/₆?").

Most standardized tests will supply several possible answers to a question and ask your child to choose the correct answer. Many tests also may include a "not given" or "none of the above" choice.

Practice Skill: Fractions and Probability

Directions: Solve each problem below.

Example:

$$\frac{2}{5} + \frac{2}{5} = \underline{\quad}$$

  Ⓐ $\frac{2}{5}$

  Ⓑ $\frac{3}{5}$

  Ⓒ $\frac{4}{5}$

  Ⓓ $\frac{0}{5}$

Answer:

  Ⓒ $\frac{4}{5}$

1 $\frac{6}{10} + \frac{3}{10} = \underline{\quad}$

  Ⓐ $\frac{9}{20}$

  Ⓑ $\frac{9}{10}$

  Ⓒ 29

  Ⓓ none of the above

2 $\frac{11}{12} - \frac{6}{12} = \underline{\quad}$

  Ⓐ $\frac{5}{24}$

  Ⓑ $\frac{17}{12}$

  Ⓒ $\frac{5}{12}$

  Ⓓ none of the above

3 Find $\frac{2}{5}$ of 10.

  Ⓐ 4

  Ⓑ 8

  Ⓒ 5

  Ⓓ none of the above

4 Multiply to find two equivalent fractions for ¹/₂.

  Ⓐ ²/₄ and ³/₆

  Ⓑ ¹/₄ and ⁴/₆

  Ⓒ ¹/₁₂ and ⁵/₁₀

  Ⓓ none of the above

5 Divide to find two equivalent fractions for ⁴/₁₂.

  Ⓐ ¹/₃ and ²/₄

  Ⓑ ¹/₃ and ²/₆

  Ⓒ ²/₁₀ and ⁴/₃

  Ⓓ none of the above

6 Write this fraction in simplest form: $^{12}/_{18}$.

   Ⓐ $^6/_9$

   Ⓑ $^4/_6$

   Ⓒ $^1/_3$

   Ⓓ none of the above

7 Arrange these fractions from largest to smallest: $^1/_5$, $^3/_5$, $^2/_5$, $^5/_5$.

   Ⓐ $^5/_5$, $^2/_5$, $^3/_5$, $^1/_5$

   Ⓑ $^1/_5$, $^3/_5$, $^2/_5$, $^5/_5$

   Ⓒ $^5/_5$, $^3/_5$, $^2/_5$, $^1/_5$

   Ⓓ none of the above

8 Which are examples of improper fractions?

   Ⓐ $^1/_4$ and $^4/_4$

   Ⓑ $^5/_5$ and $^9/_8$

   Ⓒ $^7/_8$ and $^1/_8$

   Ⓓ none of the above

9 Rename this improper fraction as a mixed number in simplest form: $^{16}/_6$.

   Ⓐ $2^2/_3$

   Ⓑ $2^4/_6$

   Ⓒ $3^1/_3$

   Ⓓ none of the above

10 The spinner is divided into 3 equal parts, with a red, yellow, and blue part. If you spin the spinner one time, what is the chance of landing on the yellow part?

   Ⓐ $^3/_3$

   Ⓑ $^1/_3$

   Ⓒ $^2/_3$

   Ⓓ none of the above

(See page 81 for answer key.)

CHAPTER 7

Decimals

There are many examples of how decimals are used in our daily lives. Children have already dealt with decimals as they use money, have their temperatures taken, check batting averages, work with calculators, or help you pump gas.

Although most fourth-grade textbooks have a separate chapter on decimals, students have already reviewed decimals as they studied place value and as they added and subtracted money values.

Comparing and ordering decimals, however, is generally a new topic in fourth grade. Although some reference has been made to the relationship between fractions and decimals, it is usually necessary to review this concept as part of an introduction to a study of decimals.

What Fourth Graders Should Know

Students entering fourth grade have had practice with both addition and subtraction of numbers involving decimals, including money problems. The process of comparing and ordering decimals is emphasized in fourth grade. Most basic math series expect students to compare and order decimals with tenths and hundredths, although those who easily grasp this concept usually will be asked to move into thousandths.

Relating fractions and decimals is emphasized in fourth grade. Students should be able to write a fraction two ways:

$7/10$ as a fraction
0.7 as a decimal

Fourth graders also should be able to compare fractions and decimals in the same problem. An example would be

$$0.5 > \tfrac{1}{4}$$

In addition, students are expected to change a mixed number to a decimal, such as

$$3 \text{ and } 80/100 = 3.80$$

and a decimal to a mixed number:

$$4.98 = 4 \text{ and } 98/100$$

Terms such as *decimal, decimal point, rounding, sum, tenth,* and *hundredths* already should be familiar to fourth-grade students. These concepts either have been used in previous years or have been introduced in earlier chapters.

What You and Your Child Can Do

Encourage your child's interest in and knowledge of decimals by talking about those you come across in your daily life.

Everyday Decimals. You might have a decimal scavenger hunt through the evening newspaper. Although most boys have a knowledge of batting averages, have you taken the time to discuss these with your daughter? Also introduce your child to the stock market listings. At the grocery store, note decimal weights showing on the electronic scale. During the Olympiads, make sure your child knows the meaning of statements such as "The skier won by two-hundredth of a second!"

Make Change. Have your child practice making change, having him count up from the cost. Make sure he begins with the smallest coins first. Have your child pay for cash purchases, and then have him count the change.

Place-Value Chart. When you make another visit to the local educational store, purchase a place-value chart, or help your child make a grid to display in his study area for reference:

hundreds tens ones.tenths hundredths thousandths

Graph It! To explore the relationship between fractions and decimals, begin with graph paper and a *new* set of colored pencils. Who can resist? Cut out 10×10 inch squares of graph paper, and have your child color 10 blocks on one, 13 blocks on another, 79 on a third, etc. If necessary, take some time to color several yourself. Then identify the fractional parts of each: $10/100$, $13/100$, $79/100$, etc. Remind your child that these also may be written as decimals: .10, .13, .79, and read as 10 hundredths, 13 hundredths, and 79 hundredths.

Decimal Cards. If you know that additional practice may be needed, write the fractions and decimals on 3×5 inch cards. Later have your child match the cards with the correct shaded graph paper.

Match Game. To help your child understand tenths, cut 2×5 inch blocks of graph paper. Again, shade in certain amounts, such as $1/10$ or 0.2. These also could be used as a matching game. For further review, spread out the graph paper and answer cards; match the cards and shaded graph paper.

Dictate It. Give your child practice by dictating questions for matching fractions and decimals. An example would be, "The fraction is 8 out of 10. What is the decimal (0.8)?" Your child may give an oral answer, or write his answer on a white board.

Use a spinner with the numbers 1 through 9 to further practice fractions and related decimals. Set up a table:

	1	2	3	4	5	6	7	8	9
Spins									
Fraction									
Decimal									

Spin the spinner 100 times, each time putting a tally mark under the correct number. When finished, total the amounts and show both the fractions and the decimals.

For reviewing decimals greater than one, or a mixed number, again begin with graph paper. Cut out 10×10 inch squares, and shade the entire area of each. Then use the partially shaded pieces from a previous activity. Have your child show you $2\frac{10}{100}$ or 2.10, $4\frac{13}{100}$ or 4.13, and $1\frac{79}{100}$ or 1.79. Read the decimals as 2 *and* 10 hundredths, 4 *and* 13 hundredths, and 1 *and* 79 hundredths. You may do a similar activity with 2×5 or 10 inch block pieces.

Number Line. In general, students have had little experience with comparing and ordering decimals before fourth grade. It is easier to have your child visualize decimals if you begin with a number line.

8.0 8.1 8.2 8.3 8.4 8.5 8.6 8.7 8.8 8.9 9.0

Using the number line, order these numbers from smallest to largest: 8.2, 8.4, 8.1, 8.8, 8.5. The answer is 8.1, 8.2, 8.4, 8.5, 8.8.

Ordering: No Number Line. Your child also should learn how to compare and order decimals without a number line. For example, compare and order 5.43, 6.78, and 5.49 from largest to smallest.

1. First compare the whole numbers (6 > 5), so 6.78 is larger than 5.43 and 5.49.

2. Then compare the tenths (.4 and .4).

3. Compare the hundredths (.43 and .49).

4. 5.49 is the larger. So the numbers are ordered 6.78, 5.49, 5.43.

Decimal Game. Use a number spinner with sections 1 through 9 to play a decimal game. Spin the spinner three times, and write the largest possible number in this form: ones . tenths, hundredths. Now each player spins three times and arranges the three numbers to be as close to the target number as possible. Each player subtracts to find the difference between his spun numbers and the target number. The winner of the round is the player whose number is closest to the target number. Declare a winner after five rounds, and spin for a new target number.

Adding and subtracting decimals is usually a review for students at this level; they typically don't experience difficulty as long as decimal points and columns are lined up. However, take some time to review rounding and estimation. For example, estimate the answer to 1.7 + 5.2. Round the 1.7 to the nearest whole number (2); round 5.2 to the nearest whole number (5). The estimated answer is 7.

What Tests May Ask

You can expect standardized tests in fourth grade to include some questions about decimals. Students may be asked to order decimals from smallest to largest and to identify which number is in the tenths or hundredths place. Tests may give a decimal and ask the child to choose its expanded form, or vice versa, and they may ask a child to convert from decimal to fraction and back. Finally, tests may present a partially shaded figure and ask (in decimals) how much of the shape is colored in.

Practice Skill: Decimals

Directions: Solve each problem below.

Example:

In the number 240.53, what number is in the *tenths* place?

Ⓐ 0

Ⓑ 5

Ⓒ 4

Ⓓ 2

Answer:

Ⓑ 5

---

1 For the number 463.7, what number is in the *tenths* place?

Ⓐ 4

Ⓑ 3

Ⓒ 7

Ⓓ 6

---

2 What is the number name for six hundred thirty-four and twenty-nine hundredths?

Ⓐ 634.029

Ⓑ 643.29

Ⓒ 634.29

Ⓓ none of the above

---

3 Order these decimals from largest to smallest: 7.8, 8.9, 7.1, 8.3.

Ⓐ   7.1, 7.8, 8.3, 8.9

Ⓑ   8.9, 8.3, 7.8, 7.1

Ⓒ   8.9, 7.8, 8.3, 7.1

Ⓓ   none of the above

4 Use either >, <, or = to compare these two decimals: 5.9 ___ 5.90.

Ⓐ   5.9 = 5.90

Ⓑ   5.9 < 5.90

Ⓒ   5.9 > 5.90

Ⓓ   none of the above

5 Write the decimal numbers for these fractions: $^{70}/_{100}$, $^{7}/_{100}$, $^{7}/_{10}$.

Ⓐ   .70, .70, .7

Ⓑ   .70, .07, .7

Ⓒ   .70, .7, .7

Ⓓ   none of the above

6 Write the fraction and the decimal for the shaded area in the figure below.

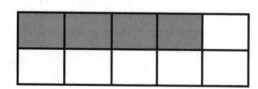

Ⓐ $^{4}/_{10}$ or .4

Ⓑ $^{4}/_{100}$ or .04

Ⓒ $^{4}/_{10}$ or .04

Ⓓ   none of the above

7 Add $36.05 and $29.64.

Ⓐ $65.68

Ⓑ   about $700

Ⓒ $64.685

Ⓓ   none of the above

8 Convert to decimals and add: $6\frac{7}{10} + 4\frac{2}{10}$.

Ⓐ   6.10 + 4.2 = 10.30

Ⓑ   6.70 + 4.02 = 10.72

Ⓒ   6.7 + 4.2 = 10.9

Ⓓ   none of the above

9 You bought a chair at a yard sale for $8.84. You gave the cashier a ten dollar bill. How much change will you receive?

Ⓐ $1.16

Ⓑ   about $1.00

Ⓒ $2.84

Ⓓ   none of the above

10 Solve the problem: 345.3 + 48.76 = ___.

Ⓐ   about 400

Ⓑ   384.79

Ⓒ   394.06

Ⓓ   none of the above

(See page 81 for answer key.)

CHAPTER 8

Standard and Metric Measurements

The topic of measurement in fourth grade includes both customary and metric activities. By this time in their school career, students usually have had many concrete experiences measuring with rulers, yardsticks and meter sticks, scales, measuring spoons, cups, and so on. They also should have had experience with conversions, but usually limited to changing inches to feet, feet to yards, cups to pints, pints to quarts, and quarts to gallons. Your child's knowledge of measurements will be deepened through problem solving, where she will need to compare and convert from unit to unit. Estimation also will be emphasized.

What Fourth Graders Should Know

Students entering fourth grade should be familiar with measuring tools and what each measures:

- Length: centimeter and inch rulers, yardsticks, meter sticks, tape measures
- Capacity or volume: containers of various sizes
- Weight: scales
- Temperature: thermometers

By the end of fourth grade, they also should be familiar with terms for each type of measurement:

- Length: *inch, foot, yard, mile, centimeter, millimeter, decimeter, meter, kilometer*
- Capacity: *fluid ounce, cup, pint, quart, gallon, milliliter, liter*

- Weight: *ounce, pound, ton, gram, kilogram*
- Temperature: *degrees Fahrenheit, degrees Celsius*

Use of the customary measurement terms probably will be a review for most fourth-grade students. However, most children at this level will not have had as many experiences with metric measurements, especially in the areas of capacity and weight.

Your child also should be able to give examples of what units of measurement to use for various objects. What are objects you would measure in inches rather than in yards? What distances would you measure in miles rather than in yards?

Most fourth graders will be comfortable with renaming customary units of length:

```
12 in     = 1 ft
3 ft      = 1 yd
1,760 yd  = 1 mi
```

However, most will need a review of customary capacity units:

```
8 fl oz = 1 c
2 c     = 1 pt
2 pt    = 1 qt
4 qt    = 1 gal
```

Renaming for weight also will have been introduced earlier in your child's school career:

```
16 oz   = 1 lb
```

Metric renamings usually are more challenging because these units are not used as commonly in the child's immediate world. Often there isn't as much time provided for the study of metrics in the school curriculum. It's common practice for most teachers to have charts of renaming tables available for easy reference.

- Length: 1 meter (m) = 100 centimeters (about as long as a baseball bat)

    1 kilometer (km) = 1,000 meters (walk around a football field 2½ times)

    1 decimeter = 10 centimeters

    10 decimeters = 1 meter

- Capacity: 1,000 milliliters (mL) = 1 liter (L)

- Weight: 1,000 grams (g) = 1 kilogram (kg)

Students are expected to solve problems involving the preceding metric terms. While some of this work will take place in math classes, practice using metric measurements also will be a part of a school's science curriculum. Most of these activities focus on hands-on types of science experiments and are used in recording observations. Fourth-grade students also are expected to understand fractional parts of units of measure, such as ⅔ of a cup or ¾ of a yard.

Since measurement estimations are so frequently used in daily living, it is important that students at this level have many opportunities to practice this skill. "About how long, about how many, about how much …" should be emphasized as much as exact measurements.

What You and Your Child Can Do

You can give your child confidence with measurement skills by providing real-life measurement activities. Make sure your child knows how to properly use and read rulers, yardsticks, meter sticks, tape measures, measuring cups, scales, and thermometers with both Fahrenheit and Celsius scales. Have your child note units of measure in everyday life, especially when metric units are used. Check the weight information on food packages such as cereal boxes. Discuss distances when you are driving; have your child estimate when you have driven a mile or 5 miles. Informally discuss what would be measured in miles, yards, feet, and inches.

Hands On! Fourth graders generally enjoy working with hands-on types of projects, such as baking cakes or deciding how to plant the flower beds. Encourage and provide projects that require exact measurements, such as poster making or building something out of wood. Although suggestions will be given here for helping your child with conversions or renaming, in general, it is the experience with hands-on measuring that is of more importance to your child's learning measurements at this level.

Scavenger Hunt. Your fourth grader will enjoy designing scavenger hunt types of measurement games for a younger sibling, such as identifying objects of a specific length or height. In the process, she is also getting some hands-on practice! If your child seems to need the actual measurement practice, give her a fun list of objects to measure:

- Length of your longest strand of hair
- Length of the rug in your room
- Width of your favorite book
- Height of your desk
- Length of your pencil

Always ask for an estimate and then an actual measurement.

Guess the Weight. Have your child arrange a group of objects from lightest to heaviest, and then check the estimates by weighing the objects with a balance scale.

Conversions. If your child seems to be challenged by renamings or conversions, begin with easier problems, such as converting feet to inches or yards to inches. Always have her use a calculator for this type of regrouping, or have a measuring tape available. Problems such as 3 yards is how many inches or 2 feet is how many inches are an appropriate way to begin.

Renaming. A fourth-grade student typically needs some guidance when first asked to solve problems involving inches *and* feet. For example, how many inches are in 5 feet, 6 inches (or $5\frac{1}{2}$ feet)? Have your child first multiply ($5 \times 12 = 60$) and then add ($60 + 6 = 66$ inches). Fourth graders sometimes are confused about what to do after the multiplication step. Emphasize that the correct operation to rename to a smaller unit is multiplication: feet to inches, yards to inches, yards to feet.

Children at this level generally find it easier to count, with a tape measure available, when renaming to a larger unit: inches to feet, inches to yards, feet to yards. Examples of this type of problem are 9 feet is how many yards, 24 inches is how many feet, and 72 inches is how many feet?

If your child seems to be challenged with renaming types of problems, make sure she is comfortable with both types, smaller to larger and larger to smaller, before mixing them. Most fourth-grade math programs also ask students to compare units. For example, 2 feet ___ 20 inches. The child should first rename the feet to inches, and then use either the larger than (>) or smaller than (<) symbol in the blank.

Card Game. Instead of using just paper and pencil types of practice, try designing a card game. Use 3×5 inch index cards, and write one of the following on each card:

1 foot	24 inches
$1\frac{1}{2}$ feet	30 inches
2 feet	36 inches
$2\frac{1}{2}$ feet	42 inches
3 feet	48 inches

$3\frac{1}{2}$ feet	54 inches
4 feet	60 inches
$4\frac{1}{2}$ feet	66 inches
5 feet	72 inches
$5\frac{1}{2}$ feet	1 yard
6 feet	2 yards
12 inches	
18 inches	

1. Mix the cards, and put them face down in a pile.
2. Players should take turns turning up two cards at a time.
3. If the two cards are equivalent, the player keeps the cards and gets a second turn.
4. If the cards are not equivalent, the player places them on the discard pile.

Adapt the rules as you wish. The discard pile could be mixed and playing could continue, or you could play for a specific amount of time. The player who has more cards at the end wins.

The same type of renaming activities may be adapted to length in metric units. If you have your child practice renaming for capacity and weight, *always* have the equivalents available for reference.

What Tests May Ask

Standardized tests may present rulers, thermometers, and other devices and ask questions about measurements to determine how well children know their facts. They may give children an example and ask how one would measure it, or ask children to estimate the size of an object. Questions will include both those which exclude and those which ask your child to choose the correct answer from among several wrong ones.

Practice Skill: Measurement

Directions: Solve each problem below.

Example:

How many inches are in 3 feet?

Ⓐ 24

Ⓑ 36

Ⓒ 12

Ⓓ 20

Answer:

Ⓑ 36

1 How many inches are in 2 feet?

Ⓐ 12 inches

Ⓑ 18 inches

Ⓒ 24 inches

Ⓓ none of the above

2 How many inches are equivalent to 3 yards?

Ⓐ 108 inches

Ⓑ 72 inches

Ⓒ 36 inches

Ⓓ none of the above

3 How many feet are equal to 2 yards?

Ⓐ 3 feet

Ⓑ 5 feet

Ⓒ 6 feet

Ⓓ none of the above

4 How many yards are equivalent to 72 inches?

Ⓐ 1 yard

Ⓑ 4 yards

Ⓒ 3 yards

Ⓓ none of the above

5 Which is longer, 10 centimeters or 1 meter?

Ⓐ 10 centimeters

Ⓑ 1 meter

Ⓒ They are equal.

6 Which is heavier, 1 pound or 16 ounces?

Ⓐ 1 pound

Ⓑ 16 ounces

Ⓒ They are equal.

7 How would you measure a football field?

Ⓐ in inches

Ⓑ in yards

Ⓒ in centimeters

Ⓓ in miles

8 What is your best estimate for the height of a fourth-grade child?

Ⓐ 50 inches

Ⓑ 50 feet

Ⓒ 10 centimeters

Ⓓ 10 millimeters

9   Which is more, 2 cups or 1 quart?

  Ⓐ   2 cups

  Ⓑ   1 quart

  Ⓒ   They are equal.

---

10   Which is less, 1,000 milliliters or 1 liter?

  Ⓐ   1,000 milliliters

  Ⓑ   1 liter

  Ⓒ   They are equal.

(See page 81 for answer key.)

CHAPTER 9

Geometry

The beginnings for the development of a child's understanding of geometry are rooted in kindergarten or even earlier. Children are provided with many opportunities to manipulate and create shapes, and they enjoy "discovering" shapes in their environment. An awareness of shapes is further developed in the primary grades as students use pattern blocks, geoboards, and attribute blocks.

Even though the study of geometry becomes more formalized at the fourth-grade level, experiences with manipulatives and concrete examples from a child's everyday environment continue to be important.

What Fourth Graders Should Know

Students entering fourth grade should be familiar with three-dimensional shapes, such as a cube, cone, cylinder, rectangular prism, triangular prism, sphere, triangular pyramid, and square pyramid. Their understanding is further developed in fourth grade by having them describe the attributes of these figures. Terms such as *flat faces, curved faces, vertex* and *vertices,* and *edges* and *curved edges* should be used as students describe the attributes of three-dimensional figures. They also should be able to list three-dimensional objects from their immediate environment that look like each of the geometric figures.

Fourth-grade students also have some background knowledge of two-dimensional objects and polygons. They have had experiences with vocabulary such as *open* and *closed figure, triangle, quadrilateral, pentagon, hexagon, octagon,* and *decagon.* They also should have some familiarity with these figures: *square, rectangle, trapezoid, parallelogram,* and *rhombus.* At the conclusion of their geometry unit in fourth grade, students should be able to demonstrate their understanding of two-dimensional figures by naming polygons and quadrilaterals and grouping these according to their attributes.

Students also have been introduced to the terms *lines, line segments,* and *rays* before entering fourth grade. After studying geometry in fourth grade, students are expected to be able to illustrate the meaning of these terms. Their descriptions should include use of the vocabulary words *endpoint, intersecting line segments, parallel lines,* and *perpendicular lines.* They also should be familiar with the term *diagonal.*

Students entering fourth grade will be familiar with the term *angle.* They will broaden their experience with angles and should be able to draw acute, obtuse, and right angles.

Somewhere in their primary-grade experience, children usually are introduced to the concept of tessellations. Some also have had experiences in art class with creating designs with tessellations. Due to schedule limitations, students do not always have time to draw their own tessellations. However, fourth-grade students should be able to show their understanding; an alternative to drawing would be to have students use pattern blocks to develop a tessellation pattern.

Most students have been introduced to the concept of congruent figures somewhere in the primary grades. At the fourth-grade level, students are expected to identify both congruent and similar figures.

Symmetry is not a new concept for students at this level. In fourth grade, students should be able to identify and draw lines of symmetry for a given figure.

One additional topic further explored in fourth grade is identifying slides, flips, and turns. These terms are usually introduced in third grade, but fourth graders are expected to be able to illustrate these terms on graph paper.

What You and Your Child Can Do

At the fourth-grade level there are many, many specialized terms related to the study of geometry. While these will be emphasized in most classrooms, you can help your child at home by creating an awareness of two- and three-dimensional figures in your immediate environment. Point out geometric figures, and help your child describe their attributes.

Geometry Scavenger Hunt. If your child is finding the study of geometric terms less than exciting, send him on a scavenger hunt around the house to locate three-dimensional objects. For example, find a rectangular prism (a cereal box), and help your child use stick-on notes to label the 12 straight edges, 6 flat faces, and 8 vertices. Or label them with a permanent magic marker. Find and label these additional three-dimensional objects:

- Cylinder (a soup can); label 2 flat faces, 1 curved face, and 2 curved edges.
- Cube (a block or a rubic cube); label 6 flat faces, 12 edges, and 8 vertices.
- Triangular pyramid (a pyramid whose base is a triangle). This isn't a common household item (your child and you may have fun shop-

ping for this one); label 4 flat faces, 6 edges, and 4 vertices.

- Square pyramid (a pyramid whose base is a square). Again, this isn't a common household item; label 5 flat faces, 8 edges, and 5 vertices.
- Triangular prism (a prism whose opposite sides are triangles); label 5 flat faces, 9 edges, and 6 vertices.
- Cone (a good excuse to go to an ice cream shop); label 1 curved face, 1 flat face, 1 curved edge, and 1 vertex.
- Sphere (a ball); label 1 curved face.

Toothpick Art. Keep a plastic bag with some toothpicks in your purse or pocket. While you're waiting (in a restaurant, in the car, or in a waiting room) ask your child to make four shapes with the toothpicks; see how many he can come up with. If there is more than one child present, stage a competition to see who can make the most shapes in 30 seconds.

Make a Model. If your child is having trouble remembering the terms for two-dimensional figures, have him make models using plastic straws and clay. Print the terms on 5 × 8 inch cards, and display the cards and figures together. (Many teachers would welcome this display in their classrooms.) Or trace the figures with a finger, one at a time, on your child's back, and have him name what you have drawn.

Tangrams. Many fourth-grade students enjoy working with tangrams (two-dimensional shapes). You can buy a plastic set at an educational store, along with books of outlined figures for your child to make. After working with tangrams, many children enjoy creating animals from the shapes. Trace the plastic tangram pieces on construction paper, cut them out, and paste the various animal shapes on background paper.

Geoboards. Another way to heighten interest in learning the names of two-dimensional figures is to make the shapes on geoboards. Play a game in which one of you makes the polygon on a geoboard; the other then names the polygon and draws a different version of the same polygon on dot paper (with longer sides or shorter sides but the same number of sides).

Shape Safari. Here's a good game to play when your child has a friend to stay. Give both children a list of geometric shapes (circle, square, rectangle, oval, triangle, polygon), together with a pad and pencil. Have each write down as many of the shapes as he can find by looking around the house—the door as a rectangle, the window as a square, the cat's head as a circle, its ears as triangles, and so on. What shape was the hardest to find? What was the most common?

Try finding shapes as you are driving down the highway. Don't just stick with the easy ones like squares and circles. Go for the rectangular prism, the pyramid, the ray, and the line segment. Look for lines that are parallel and perpendicular. Most geometry questions for children this age can be answered if the child knows what the terms mean.

What Tests May Ask

Standardized tests will ask students to identify certain shapes, give definitions of geometric terms, or select matching shape. They make ask questions about how to find perimeters and areas of figures.

Questions will ask students to find the one correct answer in a group of incorrect ones or to choose the incorrect response in a list of correct answers. There usually will be a "none of the above" statement as well.

Practice Skill: Geometry

Directions: Read each question and choose the correct answer.

Example: Choose the rectangular prism.

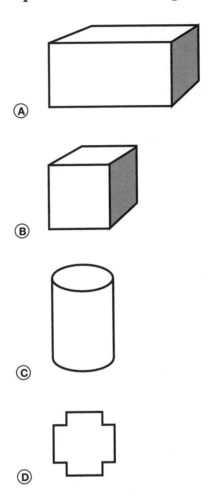

Ⓐ
Ⓑ
Ⓒ
Ⓓ

Answer:

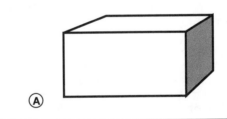

Ⓐ

---

1 A block is shaped most like a

Ⓐ   cube.

Ⓑ   cylinder.

Ⓒ   rectangular prism.

Ⓓ   sphere.

2 Which of the following shapes is a cylinder?

Ⓐ

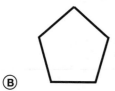
Ⓑ

Ⓒ

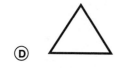
Ⓓ

3 What is the area of this shape? (Area = length × width.)

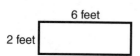

Ⓐ 36 feet

Ⓑ 12 feet

Ⓒ 36 inches

Ⓓ 48 feet

4 What angles are in the figure below?

Ⓐ right angles

Ⓑ acute angles

Ⓒ obtuse angles

Ⓓ no angles

5 Which of these is a pentagon?

Ⓐ

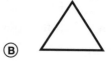
Ⓑ

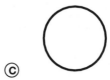
Ⓒ

Ⓓ

6 How many faces does the figure below have?

- Ⓐ 3
- Ⓑ 6
- Ⓒ 4
- Ⓓ 5

7 Line segments like the two below that stay the same distance apart from each other are called what?

- Ⓐ intersecting
- Ⓑ perpendicular
- Ⓒ parallel
- Ⓓ rays

8 The figure below is called a what?

$\longrightarrow$

- Ⓐ ray
- Ⓑ parallel line
- Ⓒ line
- Ⓓ line segment

9 The lines below are what?

- Ⓐ parallel
- Ⓑ crooked
- Ⓒ perpendicular
- Ⓓ rays

10 What is the perimeter of a square bedroom if each side is 8 feet?

- Ⓐ 16 feet
- Ⓑ 24 feet
- Ⓒ 32 feet
- Ⓓ 32 inches

(See page 81 for answer key.)

Web Sites and Resources for More Information

Homework

Homework Central
http://www.HomeworkCentral.com
Terrific site for students, parents, and teachers, filled with information, projects, and more.

Win the Homework Wars
(Sylvan Learning Centers)
http://www.educate.com/online/qa_peters.html

Reading and Grammar Help

Born to Read: How to Raise a Reader
http://www.ala.org/alsc/raise_a_reader.html

Guide to Grammar and Writing
http://webster.commnet.edu/hp/pages/darling/grammar.htm
Help with "plague words and phrases," grammar FAQs, sentence parts, punctuation, rules for common usage.

Internet Public Library: Reading Zone
http://www.ipl.org/cgi-bin/youth/youth.out

Keeping Kids Reading and Writing
http://www.tiac.net/users/maryl/

U.S. Dept. of Education: Helping Your Child Learn to Read
http://www.ed.gov/pubs/parents/Reading/index.html

Math Help

Center for Advancement of Learning
http://www.muskingum.edu/%7Ecal/database/Math2.html
Substitution and memory strategies for math.

Center for Advancement of Learning
http://www.muskingum.edu/%7Ecal/database/Math1.html
General tips and suggestions.

Math.com
http://www.math.com
The world of math online.

Math.com
http://www.math.com/student/testprep.html
Get ready for standardized tests.

Math.com: Homework Help in Math
http://www.math.com/students/homework.html

Math.com: Math for Homeschoolers
http://www.math.com/parents/homeschool.html

The Math Forum: Problems and Puzzles
http://forum.swarthmore.edu/library/resource_types/problems_puzzles
Lots of fun math puzzles and problems for grades K through 12.

The Math Forum: Math Tips and Tricks
http://forum.swarthmore.edu/k12/mathtips/mathtips.html

Tips on Testing

Books on Test Preparation
http://www.testbooksonline.com/preHS.asp
This site provides printed resources for parents who wish to help their children prepare for standardized school tests.

Core Knowledge Web Site
http://www.coreknowledge.org/
Site dedicated to providing resources for parents; based on the books of E. D. Hirsch, Jr., who wrote the *What Your X Grader Needs to Know* series.

Family Education Network
http://www.familyeducation.com/article/0,1120, 1-6219,00.html
This report presents some of the arguments against current standardized testing practices in the public schools. The site also provides links to family activities that help kids learn.

Math.com
http://www.math.com/students/testprep.html
Get ready for standardized tests.

Standardized Tests
http://arc.missouri.edu/k12/
K through 12 assessment tools and know-how.

Parents: Testing in Schools

KidSource: Talking to Your Child's Teacher about Standardized Tests
http://www.kidsource.com/kidsource/content2/ talking.assessment.k12.4.html
This site provides basic information to help parents understand their children's test results and provides pointers for how to discuss the results with their children's teachers.

eSCORE.com: State Test and Education Standards
http://www.eSCORE.com
Find out if your child meets the necessary requirements for your local schools. A Web site with experts from Brazelton Institute and Harvard's Project Zero.

Overview of States' Assessment Programs
http://ericae.net/faqs/

Parent Soup
Education Central: Standardized Tests
http://www.parentsoup.com/edcentral/testing
A parent's guide to standardized testing in the schools, written from a parent advocacy standpoint.

National Center for Fair and Open Testing, Inc. (FairTest)
342 Broadway
Cambridge, MA 02139
(617) 864-4810
http://www.fairtest.org

National Parent Information Network
http://npin.org

Publications for Parents from the U.S. Department of Education
http://www.ed.gov/pubs/parents/
An ever-changing list of information for parents available from the U.S. Department of Education.

State of the States Report
http://www.edweek.org/sreports/qc99/states/ indicators/in-intro.htm
A report on testing and achievement in the 50 states.

Testing: General Information

Academic Center for Excellence
http://www.acekids.com

American Association for Higher Education Assessment
http://www.aahe.org/assessment/web.htm

American Educational Research Association (AERA)
http://aera.net
An excellent link to reports on American education, including reports on the controversy over standardized testing.

American Federation of Teachers
555 New Jersey Avenue, NW
Washington, D.C. 20011

Association of Test Publishers Member Products and Services
http://www.testpublishers.org/memserv.htm

Education Week on the Web
http://www.edweek.org

ERIC Clearinghouse on Assessment and Evaluation
1131 Shriver Lab
University of Maryland
College Park, MD 20742
http://ericae.net
A clearinghouse of information on assessment and education reform.

FairTest: The National Center for Fair and Open Testing
http://fairtest.org/facts/ntfact.htm
http://fairtest.org/
The National Center for Fair and Open Testing is an advocacy organization working to end the abuses, misuses, and flaws of standardized testing and to ensure that evaluation of students and workers is fair, open, and educationally sound. This site provides many links to fact sheets, opinion papers, and other sources of information about testing.

National Congress of Parents and Teachers
700 North Rush Street
Chicago, Illinois 60611

National Education Association
1201 16th Street, NW
Washington, DC 20036

National School Boards Association
http://www.nsba.org
A good source for information on all aspects of public education, including standardized testing.

Testing Our Children: A Report Card on State Assessment Systems
http://www.fairtest.org/states/survey.htm
Report of testing practices of the states, with graphical links to the states and a critique of fair testing practices in each state.

Trends in Statewide Student Assessment Programs: A Graphical Summary
http://www.ccsso.org/survey96.html
Results of annual survey of states' departments of public instruction regarding their testing practices.

U.S. Department of Education
http://www.ed.gov/

Web Links for Parents Who Want to Help Their Children Achieve
http://www.liveandlearn.com/learn.html
This page offers many Web links to free and for-sale information and materials for parents who want to help their children do well in school. Titles include such free offerings as the Online Colors Game and questionnaires to determine whether your child is ready for school.

What Should Parents Know about Standardized Testing in the Schools?
http://www.rusd.k12.ca.us/parents/standard.html
An online brochure about standardized testing in the schools, with advice regarding how to become an effective advocate for your child.

Test Publishers Online

ACT: Information for Life's Transitions
http://www.act.org

American Guidance Service, Inc.
http://www.agsnet.com

Ballard & Tighe Publishers
http://www.ballard-tighe.com

Consulting Psychologists Press
http://www.cpp-db.com

CTB McGraw-Hill
http://www.ctb.com

Educational Records Bureau
http://www.erbtest.org/index.html

Educational Testing Service
http://www.ets.org

General Educational Development (GED) Testing Service
http://www.acenet.edu/calec/ged/home.html

Harcourt Brace Educational Measurement
http://www.hbem.com

Piney Mountain Press—A Cyber-Center for Career and Applied Learning
http://www.pineymountain.com

ProEd Publishing
http://www.proedinc.com

Riverside Publishing Company
http://www.hmco.com/hmco/riverside

Stoelting Co.
http://www.stoeltingco.com

Sylvan Learning Systems, Inc.
http://www.educate.com

Touchstone Applied Science Associates, Inc. (TASA)
http://www.tasa.com

Tests Online

(*Note:* We don't endorse tests; some may not have technical documentation. Evaluate the quality of any testing program before making decisions based on its use.)

Edutest, Inc.
http://www.edutest.com
Edutest is an Internet-accessible testing service that offers criterion-referenced tests for elementary school students, based upon the standards for K through 12 learning and achievement in the states of Virginia, California, and Florida.

Virtual Knowledge
http://www.smarterkids.com
This commercial service, which enjoys a formal partnership with Sylvan Learning Centers, offers a line of skills assessments for preschool through grade 9 for use in the classroom or the home. For free online sample tests, see the Virtual Test Center.

Read More about It

Abbamont, Gary W. *Test Smart: Ready-to-Use Test-Taking Strategies and Activities for Grades 5–12.* Upper Saddle River, NJ: Prentice Hall Direct, 1997.

Cookson, Peter W., and Joshua Halberstam. *A Parent's Guide to Standardized Tests in School: How to Improve Your Child's Chances for Success.* New York: Learning Express, 1998.

Frank, Steven, and Stephen Frank. *Test-Taking Secrets: Study Better, Test Smarter, and Get Great Grades (The Backpack Study Series).* Holbrook, MA: Adams Media Corporation, 1998.

Gilbert, Sara Dulaney. *How to Do Your Best on Tests: A Survival Guide.* New York: Beech Tree Books, 1998.

Gruber, Gary. *Dr. Gary Gruber's Essential Guide to Test-Taking for Kids, Grades 3–5.* New York: William Morrow & Co., 1986.

———. *Gary Gruber's Essential Guide to Test-Taking for Kids, Grades 6, 7, 8, 9.* New York: William Morrow & Co., 1997.

Leonhardt, Mary. *99 Ways to Get Kids to Love Reading and 100 Books They'll Love.* New York: Crown, 1997.

———. *Parents Who Love Reading, Kids Who Don't: How It Happens and What You Can Do about It.* New York: Crown, 1995.

McGrath, Barbara B. *The Baseball Counting Book.* Watertown, MA: Charlesbridge, 1999.

———. *More M&M's Brand Chocolate Candies Math.* Watertown, MA: Charlesbridge, 1998.

Mokros, Janice R. *Beyond Facts & Flashcards: Exploring Math with Your Kids.* Portsmouth, NH: Heinemann, 1996.

Romain, Trevor, and Elizabeth Verdick. *True or False?: Tests Stink!* Minneapolis: Free Spirit Publishing Co., 1999.

Schartz, Eugene M. *How to Double Your Child's Grades in School: Build Brilliance and Leadership into Your Child—from Kindergarten to College—in Just 5 Minutes a Day.* New York: Barnes & Noble, 1999.

Taylor, Kathe, and Sherry Walton. *Children at the Center: A Workshop Approach to Standardized Test Preparation, K–8.* Portsmouth, NH: Heinemann, 1998.

Tobia, Sheila. *Overcoming Math Anxiety.* New York: W. W. Norton & Company, Inc., 1995.

Tufariello, Ann Hunt. *Up Your Grades: Proven Strategies for Academic Success.* Lincolnwood, IL: VGM Career Horizons, 1996.

Vorderman, Carol. *How Math Works.* Pleasantville, NY: Reader's Digest Association, Inc., 1996.

Zahler, Kathy A. *50 Simple Things You Can Do to Raise a Child Who Loves to Read.* New York: IDG Books, 1997.

What Your Child's Test Scores Mean

Several weeks or months after your child has taken standardized tests, you will receive a report such as the TerraNova Home Report found in Figures 1 and 2. You will receive similar reports if your child has taken other tests. We briefly examine what information the reports include.

Look at the first page of the Home Report. Note that the chart provides labeled bars showing the child's performance. Each bar is labeled with the child's National Percentile for that skill area. When you know how to interpret them, national percentiles can be the most useful scores you encounter on reports such as this. Even when you are confronted with different tests that use different scale scores, you can always interpret percentiles the same way, regardless of the test. A percentile tells the percent of students who score at or below that level. A percentile of 25, for example, means that 25 percent of children taking the test scored at or below that score. (It also means that 75 percent of students scored above that score.) Note that the average is always at the 50th percentile.

On the right side of the graph on the first page of the report, the publisher has designated the ranges of scores that constitute average, above average, and below average. You can also use this slightly more precise key for interpreting percentiles:

PERCENTILE RANGE	LEVEL
2 and Below	Deficient
3–8	Borderline
9–23	Low Average
24–75	Average
76–97	High Average
98 and Up	Superior

The second page of the Home report provides a listing of the child's strengths and weaknesses, along with keys for mastery, partial mastery, and non-mastery of the skills. Scoring services determine these breakdowns based on the child's scores as compared with those from the national norm group.

Your child's teacher or guidance counselor will probably also receive a profile report similar to the TerraNova Individual Profile Report, shown in Figures 3 and 4. That report will be kept in your child's permanent record. The first aspect of this report to notice is that the scores are expressed both numerically and graphically.

First look at the score bands under National Percentile. Note that the scores are expressed as bands, with the actual score represented by a dot within each band. The reason we express the scores as bands is to provide an idea of the amount by which typical scores may vary for each student. That is, each band represents a

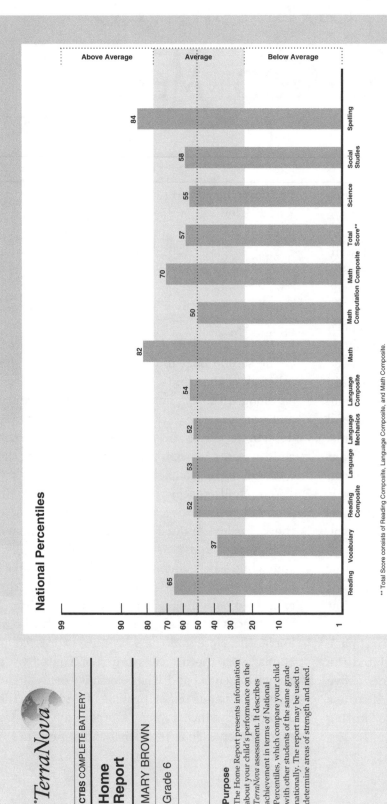

Figure 1 (SOURCE: CTB/McGraw-Hill, copyright © 1997. All rights reserved. Reproduced with permission.)

TerraNova

CTBS COMPLETE BATTERY

Home Report

MARY BROWN

Grade 6

Purpose

This page of the Home Report presents information about your child's strengths and needs. This information is provided to help you monitor your child's academic growth.

Simulated Data

Birthdate: 02/08/85
Special Codes:
A B C D E F G H I J K L M N O P Q R S T
3 5 9 7 3 2   1 1 1
Form/Level: A-16
Test Date: 11/01/99   Scoring: PATTERN (IRT)
QM: 08   Norms Date: 1996

Class: PARKER
School: WINFIELD
District: WINFIELD

City/State: WINFIELD, CA

McGraw-Hill

Page 2

Strengths

Reading
● Basic Understanding
● Analyze Text

Vocabulary
● Word Meaning
● Words in Context

Language
● Editing Skills
● Sentence Structure

Language Mechanics
● Sentences, Phrases, Clauses

Mathematics
● Computation and Numerical Estimation
● Operation Concepts

Mathematics Computation
● Add Whole Numbers
● Multiply Whole Numbers

Science
● Life Science
● Inquiry Skills

Social Studies
● Geographic Perspectives
● Economic Perspectives

Spelling
● Vowels
● Consonants

Key ● Mastery

General Interpretation

The left column shows your child's best areas of performance. In each case, your child has reached mastery level. The column at the right shows the areas within each test section where your child's scores are the lowest. In these cases, your child has not reached mastery level, although he or she may have reached partial mastery.

Needs

Reading
◑ Evaluate and Extend Meaning
○ Identify Reading Strategies

Vocabulary
○ Multimeaning Words

Language
◑ Writing Strategies

Language Mechanics
○ Writing Conventions

Mathematics
◑ Measurement
○ Geometry and Spatial Sense

Mathematics Computation
○ Percents

Science
○ Earth and Space Science

Social Studies
◑ Historical and Cultural Perspectives

Spelling
No area of needs were identified for this content area

Key ◑ Partial Mastery   ○ Non-Mastery

Figure 2   (SOURCE: CTB/McGraw-Hill, copyright © 1997. All rights reserved. Reproduced with permission.)

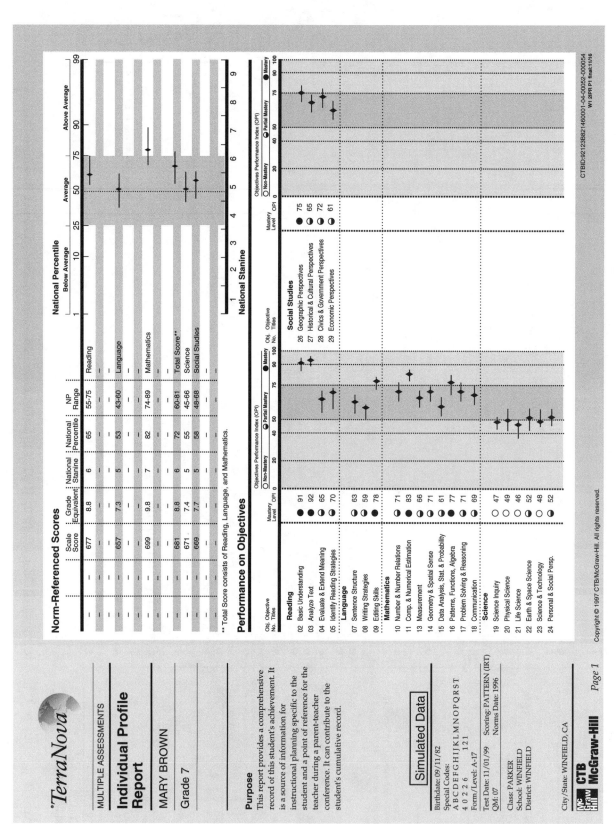

Figure 3 (SOURCE: CTB/McGraw-Hill, copyright © 1997. All rights reserved. Reproduced with permission.)

Observations

Norm-Referenced Scores

The top section of the report presents information about this student's achievement in several different ways. The National Percentile (NP) data and graph indicate how this student performed compared to students of the same grade nationally. The National Percentile range indicates that if this student had taken the test numerous times the scores would have fallen within the range shown. The shaded area on the graph represents the average range of scores, usually defined as the middle 50 percent of students nationally. Scores in the area to the right of the shading are above the average range. Scores in the area to the left of the shading are below the average range.

In Reading, for example, this student achieved a National Percentile rank of 65. This student scored higher than 65 percent of the students nationally. This score is in the average range. This student has a total of five scores in the average range. One score is in the above average range. No scores are in the below average range.

Performance on Objectives

The next section of the report presents performance on the objectives. Each objective is measured by a minimum of 4 items. The Objectives Performance Index (OPI) provides an estimate of the number of items that a student could be expected to answer correctly if there had been 100 items for that objective. The OPI is used to indicate mastery of each objective. An OPI of 75 and above characterizes Mastery. An OPI between 50 and 74 indicates Partial Mastery, and an OPI below 50 indicates Non-Mastery. The two-digit number preceding the objective title identifies the objective, which is fully described in the Teacher's Guide to *TerraNova*. The bands on either side of the diamonds indicate the range within which the student's test scores would fall if the student were tested numerous times.

In Reading, for example, this student could be expected to respond correctly to 91 out of 100 items measuring Basic Understanding. If this student had taken the test numerous times the OPI for this objective would have fallen between 82 and 93.

Teacher Notes

TerraNova

MULTIPLE ASSESSMENTS

Individual Profile Report

MARY BROWN

Grade 7

Purpose

The Observations section of the Individual Profile Report gives teachers and parents information to interpret this report. This page is a narrative description of the data on the other side.

Simulated Data

Birthdate: 09/11/82
Special Codes:
A B C D E F G H I J K L M N O P Q R S T
4 0 2 2 6   1 2 1
Form/Level: A-17

Test Date: 11/01/99   Scoring: PATTERN (IRT)
QM: 08   Norms Date: 1996

Class: PARKER
School: WINFIELD
District: WINFIELD

City/State: WINFIELD, CA

 CTB
McGraw-Hill   *Page 2*

Figure 4

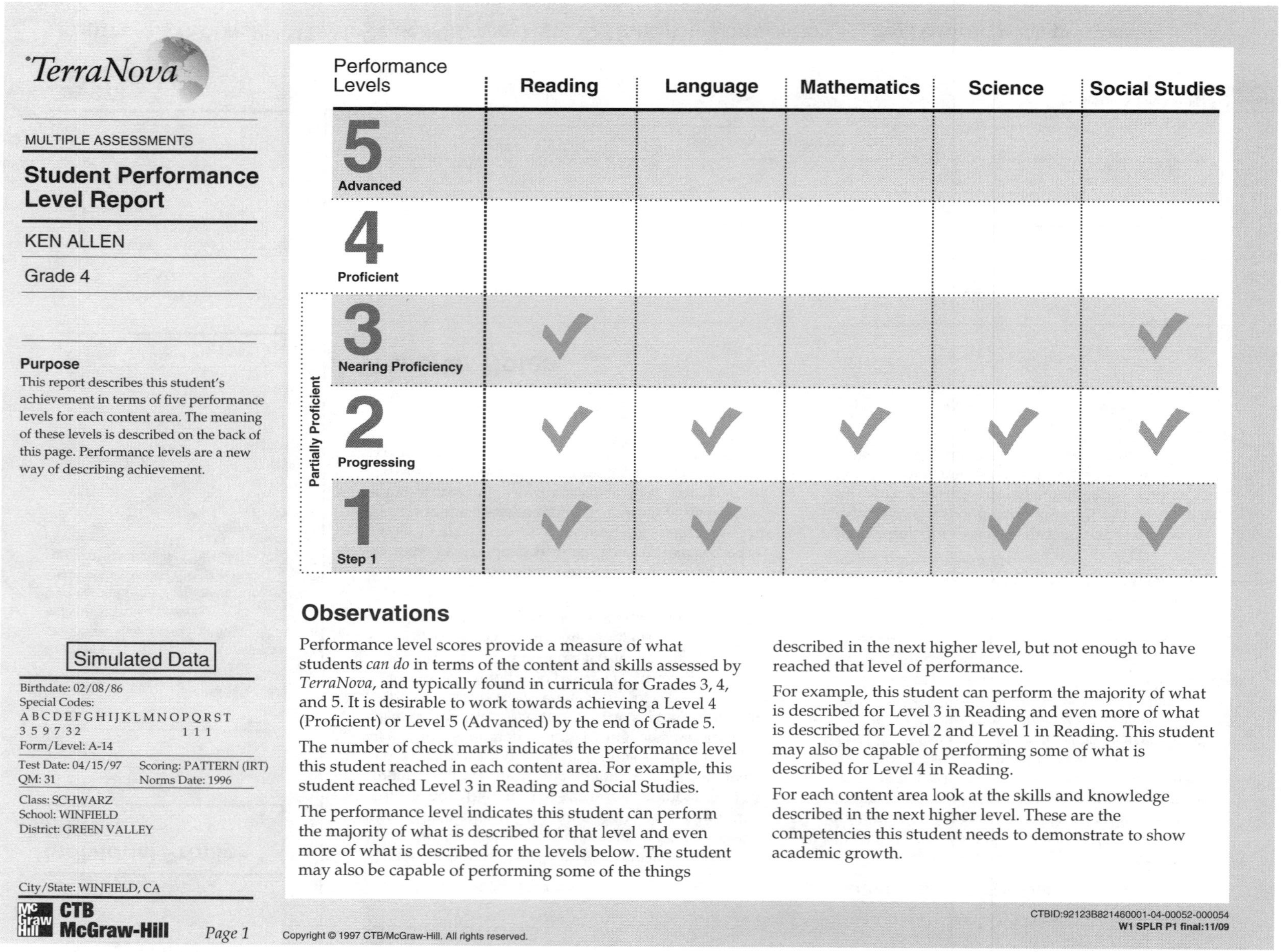

Figure 5 (SOURCE: CTB/McGraw-Hill, copyright © 1997. All rights reserved. Reproduced with permission.)

Performance Levels (Grades 3, 4, 5)	Reading	Language	Mathematics	Science	Social Studies
5 Advanced	Students use analogies to generalize. They identify a paraphrase of concepts or ideas in texts. They can indicate thought processes that led them to a previous answer. In written responses, they demonstrate understanding of an implied theme, assess intent of passage information, and provide justification as well as support for their answers.	Students understand logical development in paragraph structure. They identify essential information from notes. They recognize the effect of prepositional phrases on subject-verb agreement. They find and correct at least 4 out of 6 errors when editing simple narratives. They correct run-on and incomplete sentences in more complex texts. They can eliminate all errors when editing their own work.	Students locate decimals on a number line; compute with decimals and fractions; read scale drawings; find areas; identify geometric transformations; construct and label bar graphs; find simple probabilities; find averages; use patterns in data to solve problems; use multiple strategies and concepts to solve unfamiliar problems; express mathematical ideas and explain the problem-solving process.	Students understand a broad range of grade level scientific concepts, such as the structure of Earth and instinctive behavior. They know terminology, such as decomposers, fossil fuel, eclipse, and buoyancy. Knowledge of more complex environmental issues includes, for example, the positive consequences of a forest fire. Students can process and interpret more detailed tables and graphs. They can suggest improvements to experimental design, such as running more trials.	Students consistently demonstrate skills such as synthesizing information from two sources (e.g., a document and a map). They show understanding of the democratic process and global environmental issues, and know the location of continents and major countries. They analyze and summarize information from multiple sources in early American history. They thoroughly explain both sides of an issue and give complete and detailed written answers to questions.
4 Proficient	Students interpret figures of speech. They recognize paraphrase of text information and retrieve information to complete forms. In more complex texts, they identify themes, main ideas, or author purpose/point of view. They analyze and apply information in graphic and text form, make reasonable generalizations, and draw conclusions. In written responses, they can identify key elements from text.	Students select the best supporting sentence for a topic sentence. They use compound predicates to combine sentences. They identify simple subjects and predicates, recognize correct usage when confronted with two types of errors, and find and correct at least 3 out of 6 errors when editing simple narratives. They can edit their own work with only minor errors.	Students compare, order, and round whole numbers; know place value to thousands; identify fractions; use computation and estimation strategies; relate multiplication to addition; measure to nearest half-inch and centimeter; measure and find perimeters; estimate measures; find elapsed times; combine and subdivide shapes; identify parallel lines; interpret tables and graphs; solve two-step problems.	Students have a range of specific science knowledge, including details about animal adaptations and classification, states of matter, and the geology of Earth. They recognize scientific words such as habitat, gravity, and mass. They understand the usefulness of computers. They understand reasons for conserving natural resources. Understanding of experimentation includes analyzing purpose, interpreting data, and selecting tools to gather data.	Students demonstrate skills such as making inferences, using historical documents and analyzing maps to determine the economic strengths of a region. They understand the function of currency in various cultures and supply and demand. They summarize information from multiple sources, determine relationships, determine relevance of information, and show global awareness. They propose solutions to real-world problems and support ideas with appropriate details.
3 Nearing Proficiency	Students use context clues and structural analysis to determine word meaning. They recognize homonyms and antonyms in grade-level text. They identify important details, sequence, cause and effect, and lessons embedded in the text. They interpret characters' feelings and apply information to new situations. In written responses, they can express an opinion and support it.	Students identify irrelevant sentences in paragraphs and select the best place to insert new information. They recognize faulty sentence construction. They can combine simple sentences with conjunctions and use simple subordination of phrases/clauses. They identify reference sources. They recognize correct conventions for dates, closings, and place names in informal correspondence.	Students identify even and odd numbers; subtract whole numbers with regrouping; multiply and divide by one-digit numbers; identify simple fractions; measure with ruler to nearest inch; tell time to nearest fifteen minutes; recognize and classify common shapes; recognize symmetry; subdivide shapes; complete bar graphs; extend numerical and geometric patterns; apply simple logical reasoning.	Students are familiar with the life cycles of plants and animals. They can identify an example of a cold-blooded animal. They infer what once existed from fossil evidence. They recognize the term habitat. They understand the water cycle. They know science and sources of pollution. They can sequence life in different times and understand some economic concepts related to products, jobs, and the environment. They give some detail in written responses.	Students demonstrate skills in organizing information. They use time lines, product and global maps, and cardinal directions. They understand simple cause and effect relationships and historical documents. They sequence events, associate holidays with events, and classify natural resources. They compare life in different times and understand some economic concepts related to products, jobs, and the environment. They give some detail in written responses.
2 Progressing	Students identify synonyms for grade-level words, and use context clues to define common words. They make simple inferences and predictions based on text. They identify characters' feelings. They can transfer information from text to graphic form, or from graphic form to text. In written responses, they can provide limited support for their answers.	Students identify the use of correct verb tenses and supply verbs to complete sentences. They complete paragraphs by selecting an appropriate topic sentence. They select correct adjective forms.	Students know ordinal numbers; solve coin combination problems; count by tens; add whole numbers with regrouping; have basic estimation skills; understand addition property of zero; write and identify number sentences describing simple situations; read calendars; identify appropriate measurement tools; recognize congruent figures; use simple coordinate grids; read common tables and graphs.	Students recognize that plants decompose and become part of soil. They can classify a plant as a vegetable. They recognize that camouflage relates to survival. They recognize terms such as hibernate. They have an understanding of human impact on the environment and are familiar with causes of pollution. They find the correct bar graph to represent given data and transfer data appropriate for middle elementary grades to a bar graph.	Students demonstrate simple information-processing skills such as using basic maps and keys. They recognize simple geographical terms, types of jobs, modes of transportation, and natural resources. They connect a human need with an appropriate community service. They identify some early famous presidents and know the capital of the United States. Their written answers are partially complete.
1 Step 1	Students select pictured representations of ideas and identify stated details contained in simple texts. In written responses, they can select and transfer information from charts.	Students supply subjects to complete sentences. They identify the correct use of pronouns. They make edits for the correct use of end marks and initial capital letters, and identify the correct convention for greetings in letters.	Students read and recognize numbers to 1000; identify real-world use of numbers; add and subtract two-digit numbers without regrouping; identify addition situations; recognize and complete simple geometric and numerical patterns.	Students recognize basic science adaptations for living in the water, identify an animal that is hatched from an egg, and associate an organism with its correct environment. They identify an object as metal. They have some understanding of conditions on the moon. They supply one way a computer can be useful. They associate an instrument like a telescope with a field of study.	Students are developing fundamental social studies skills such as locating and classifying basic information. They locate information in pictures and read and complete simple bar graphs related to social studies concepts and contexts. They can connect some city buildings with their functions and recognize certain historical objects.

Partially Proficient

IMPORTANT: Each performance level, depicted on the other side, indicates the student can perform the majority of what is described for that level and even more of what is described for the levels below. The student may also be capable of performing some of the things described in the next higher level, but not enough to have reached that level.

Figure 6 (SOURCE: CTB/McGraw-Hill, copyright © 1997. All rights reserved. Reproduced with permission.)

confidence interval. In these reports, we usually report either a 90 percent or 95 percent confidence interval. Interpret a confidence interval this way: Suppose we report a 90 percent confidence interval of 25 to 37. This means we estimate that, if the child took the test multiple times, we would expect that child's score to be in the 25 to 37 range 90 percent of the time.

Now look under the section titled Norm-Referenced Scores on the first page of the Individual Profile Report (Figure 3). The farthest column on the right provides the NP Range, which is the National Percentile scores represented by the score bands in the chart.

Next notice the column labeled Grade Equivalent. Theoretically, grade level equivalents equate a student's score in a skill area with the average grade placement of children who made the same score. Many psychologists and test developers would prefer that we stopped reporting grade equivalents, because they can be grossly misleading. For example, the average reading grade level of high school seniors as reported by one of the more popular tests is the eighth grade level. Does that mean that the nation's high school seniors cannot read? No. The way the test publisher calculated grade equivalents was to determine the average test scores for students in grades 4 to 6 and then simply extend the resulting prediction formula to grades 7 to 12. The result is that parents of average high school seniors who take the test in question would mistakenly believe that their seniors are reading four grade levels behind! Stick to the percentile in interpreting your child's scores.

Now look at the columns labeled Scale Score and National Stanine. These are two of a group of scores we also call *standard scores.* In reports for other tests, you may see other standard scores reported, such as Normal Curve Equivalents (NCEs), Z-Scores, and T-Scores. The IQ that we report on intelligence tests, for example, is a standard score. Standard scores are simply a way of expressing a student's scores in terms of the statistical properties of the scores from the norm group against which we are comparing the child. Although most psychologists prefer to speak in terms of standard scores among themselves, parents are advised to stick to percentiles in interpreting your child's performance.

Now look at the section of the report labeled Performance on Objectives. In this section, the test publisher reports how your child did on the various skills that make up each skills area. Note that the scores on each objective are expressed as a percentile band, and you are again told whether your child's score constitutes mastery, non-mastery, or partial mastery. Note that these scores are made up of tallies of sometimes small numbers of test items taken from sections such as Reading or Math. Because they are calculated from a much smaller number of scores than the main scales are (for example, Sentence Comprehension is made up of fewer items than overall Reading), their scores are less reliable than those of the main scales.

Now look at the second page of the Individual Profile Report (Figure 4). Here the test publisher provides a narrative summary of how the child did on the test. These summaries are computer-generated according to rules provided by the publisher. Note that the results descriptions are more general than those on the previous three report pages. But they allow the teacher to form a general picture of which students are performing at what general skill levels.

Finally, your child's guidance counselor may receive a summary report such as the TerraNova Student Performance Level Report. (See Figures 5 and 6.) In this report, the publisher explains to school personnel what skills the test assessed and generally how proficiently the child tested under each skill.

Which States Require Which Tests

Tables 1 through 3 summarize standardized testing practices in the 50 states and the District of Columbia. This information is constantly changing; the information presented here was accurate as of the date of printing of this book. Many states have changed their testing practices in response to revised accountability legislation, while others have changed the tests they use.

Table 1   State Web Sites: Education and Testing

STATE	GENERAL WEB SITE	STATE TESTING WEB SITE
Alabama	http://www.alsde.edu/	http://www.fairtest.org/states/al.htm
Alaska	www.educ.state.ak.us/	http://www.educ.state.ak.us/
Arizona	http://www.ade.state.az.us/	http://www.ade.state.az.us/standards/
Arkansas	http://arkedu.k12.ar.us/	http://www.fairtest.org/states/ar.htm
California	http://goldmine.cde.ca.gov/	http://star.cde.ca.gov/
Colorado	http://www.cde.state.co.us/index_home.htm	http://www.cde.state.co.us/index_assess.htm
Connecticut	http://www.state.ct.us/sde/	http://www.state.ct.us/sde/cmt/index.htm
Delaware	http://www.doe.state.de.us/	http://www.doe.state.de.us/aab/index.htm
District of Columbia	http://www.k12.dc.us/dcps/home.html	http://www.k12.dc.us/dcps/data/data_frame2.html
Florida	http://www.firn.edu/doe/	http://www.firn.edu/doe/sas/sasshome.htm
Georgia	http://www.doe.k12.ga.us/	http://www.doe.k12.ga.us/sla/ret/recotest.html
Hawaii	http://kalama.doe.hawaii.edu/upena/	http://www.fairtest.org/states/hi.htm
Idaho	http://www.sde.state.id.us/Dept/	http://www.sde.state.id.us/instruct/ schoolaccount/statetesting.htm
Illinois	http://www.isbe.state.il.us/	http://www.isbe.state.il.us/isat/
Indiana	http://doe.state.in.us/	http://doe.state.in.us/assessment/welcome.html
Iowa	http://www.state.ia.us/educate/index.html	(Tests Chosen Locally)
Kansas	http://www.ksbe.state.ks.us/	http://www.ksbe.state.ks.us/assessment/
Kentucky	http://www.kde.state.ky.us/	http://www.kde.state.ky.us/oaa/
Louisiana	http://www.doe.state.la.us/DOE/asps/home.asp	http://www.doe.state.la.us/DOE/asps/home.asp? I=HISTAKES
Maine	http://janus.state.me.us/education/homepage.htm	http://janus.state.me.us/education/mea/ meacompass.htm
Maryland	http://www.msde.state.md.us/	http://msp.msde.state.md.us/
Massachusetts	http://www.doe.mass.edu/	http://www.doe.mass.edu/mcas/
Michigan	http://www.mde.state.mi.us/	http://www.MeritAward.state.mi.us/merit/meap/ index.htm

STATE	GENERAL WEB SITE	STATE TESTING WEB SITE
Minnesota	http://www.educ.state.mn.us/	http://fairtest.org/states/mn.htm
Mississippi	http://mdek12.state.ms.us/	http://fairtest.org/states/ms.htm
Missouri	http://services.dese.state.mo.us/	http://fairtest.org/states/mo.htm
Montana	http://www.metnet.state.mt.us/	http://fairtest.org/states/mt.htm
Nebraska	http://www.nde.state.ne.us/	http://www.edneb.org/IPS/AppAccrd/ApprAccrd.html
Nevada	http://www.nde.state.nv.us/	http://www.nsn.k12.nv.us/nvdoe/reports/TerraNova.doc
New Hampshire	http://www.state.nh.us/doe/	http://www.state.nh.us/doe/Assessment/assessme(NHEIAP).htm
New Jersey	http://www.state.nj.us/education/	http://www.state.nj.us/njded/stass/index.html
New Mexico	http://sde.state.nm.us/	http://sde.state.nm.us/press/august30a.html
New York	http://www.nysed.gov/	http://www.emsc.nysed.gov/ciai/assess.html
North Carolina	http://www.dpi.state.nc.us/	http://www.dpi.state.nc.us/accountability/reporting/index.html
North Dakota	http://www.dpi.state.nd.us/dpi/index.htm	http://www.dpi.state.nd.us/dpi/reports/assess/assess.htm
Ohio	http://www.ode.state.oh.us/	http://www.ode.state.oh.us/ca/
Oklahoma	http://sde.state.ok.us/	http://sde.state.ok.us/acrob/testpack.pdf
Oregon	http://www.ode.state.or.us//	http://www.ode.state.or.us//asmt/index.htm
Pennsylvania	http://www.pde.psu.edu/	http://www.fairtest.org/states/pa.htm
Rhode Island	http://www.ridoe.net/	http://www.ridoe.net/standards/default.htm
South Carolina	http://www.state.sc.us/sde/	http://www.state.sc.us/sde/reports/terranov.htm
South Dakota	http://www.state.sd.us/state/executive/deca/	http://www.state.sd.us/state/executive/deca/TA/McRelReport/McRelReports.htm
Tennessee	http://www.state.tn.us/education/	http://www.state.tn.us/education/tsintro.htm
Texas	http://www.tea.state.tx.us/	http://www.tea.state.tx.us/student.assessment/
Utah	http://www.usoe.k12.ut.us/	http://www.usoe.k12.ut.us/eval/usoeeval.htm
Vermont	http://www.state.vt.us/educ/	http://www.fairtest.org/states/vt.htm

STATE	GENERAL WEB SITE	STATE TESTING WEB SITE
Virginia	http://www.pen.k12.va.us/Anthology/VDOE/	http://www.pen.k12.va.us/VDOE/Assessment/home.shtml
Washington	http://www.k12.wa.us/	http://www.k12.wa.us/assessment/
West Virginia	http://wvde.state.wv.us/	http://wvde.state.wv.us/
Wisconsin	http://www.dpi.state.wi.us/	http://www.dpi.state.wi.us/dpi/dltcl/eis/achfacts.html
Wyoming	http://www.k12.wy.us/wdehome.html	http://www.asme.com/wycas/index.htm

Table 2 Norm-Referenced and Criterion-Referenced Tests Administered by State

STATE	NORM-REFERENCED TEST	CRITERION-REFERENCED TEST	EXIT EXAM
Alabama	Stanford Achievement Test		Alabama High School Graduation Exam
Alaska	California Achievement Test	Alaska Benchmark Examinations	
Arizona	Stanford Achievement Test	Arizona's Instrument to Measure Standards (AIMS)	
Arkansas	Stanford Achievement Test		
California	Stanford Achievement Test	Standardized Testing and Reporting Supplement	High School Exit Exam (HSEE)
Colorado	None	Colorado Student Assessment Program	
Connecticut		Connecticut Mastery Test	
Delaware	Stanford Achievement Test	Delaware Student Testing Program	
District of Columbia	Stanford Achievement Test		
Florida	(Locally Selected)	Florida Comprehensive Assessment Test (FCAT)	High School Competency Test (HSCT)
Georgia	Stanford Achievement Test	Georgia Kindergarten Assessment Program—Revised and Criterion-Referenced Competency Tests (CRCT)	Georgia High School Graduation Tests
Hawaii	Stanford Achievement Test	Credit by Examination	Hawaii State Test of Essential Competencies
Idaho	Iowa Tests of Basic Skills/ Tests of Achievement and Proficiency	Direct Writing/Mathematics Assessment, Idaho Reading Indicator	
Illinois		Illinois Standards Achievement Tests	Prairie State Achievement Examination
Indiana		Indiana Statewide Testing for Educational Progress	
Iowa	(None)		
Kansas		(State-Developed Tests)	
Kentucky	Comprehensive Test of Basic Skills	Kentucky Core Content Tests	
Louisiana	Iowa Tests of Basic Skills	Louisiana Educational Assessment Program	Graduate Exit Exam
Maine		Maine Educational Assessment	High School Assessment Test
Maryland		Maryland School Performance Assessment Program, Maryland Functional Testing Program	

STATE	NORM-REFERENCED TEST	CRITERION-REFERENCED TEST	EXIT EXAM
Massachusetts		Massachusetts Comprehensive Assessment System	
Michigan		Michigan Educational Assessment Program	High School Test
Minnesota		Basic Standards Test	Profile of Learning
Mississippi	Comprehensive Test of Basic Skills	Subject Area Testing Program	Functional Literacy Examination
Missouri		Missouri Mastery and Achievement Test	
Montana	Iowa Tests of Basic Skills		
Nebraska			
Nevada	TerraNova		Nevada High School Proficiency Examination
New Hampshire		NH Educational Improvement and Assessment Program	
New Jersey		Elementary School Proficiency Test/Early Warning Test	High School Proficiency Test
New Mexico	TerraNova		New Mexico High School Competency Exam
New York		Pupil Evaluation Program/ Preliminary Competency Tests	Regents Competency Tests
North Carolina	Iowa Tests of Basic Skills	NC End of Grade Test	
North Dakota	TerraNova	ND Reading, Writing, Speaking, Listening, Math Test	
Ohio		Ohio Proficiency Tests	Ohio Proficiency Tests
Oklahoma	Iowa Tests of Basic Skills	Oklahoma Criterion- Referenced Tests	
Oregon		Oregon Statewide Assessment	
Pennsylvania		Pennsylvania System of School Assessment	
Rhode Island	Metropolitan Achievement Test	New Standards English Language Arts Reference Exam, New Standards Mathematics Reference Exam, Rhode Island Writing Assessment, and Rhode Island Health Education Assessment	
South Carolina	TerraNova	Palmetto Achievement Challenge Tests	High School Exit Exam
South Dakota	Stanford Achievement Test		
Tennessee	Tennessee Comprehensive Assessment Program	Tennessee Comprehensive Assessment Program	

STATE	NORM-REFERENCED TEST	CRITERION-REFERENCED TEST	EXIT EXAM
Texas		Texas Assessment of Academic Skills, End-of-Course Examinations	Texas Assessment of Academic Skills
Utah	Stanford Achievement Test	Core Curriculum Testing	
Vermont		New Standards Reference Exams	
Virginia	Stanford Achievement Test	Virginia Standards of Learning	Virginia Standards of Learning
Washington	Iowa Tests of Basic Skills	Washington Assessment of Student Learning	Washington Assessment of Student Learning
West Virginia	Stanford Achievement Test		
Wisconsin	TerraNova	Wisconsin Knowledge and Concepts Examinations	
Wyoming	TerraNova	Wyoming Comprehensive Assessment System	Wyoming Comprehensive Assessment System

Table 3   Standardized Test Schedules by State

STATE	KG	1	2	3	4	5	6	7	8	9	10	11	12	COMMENT
Alabama				X	X	X	X	X	X	X	X	X	X	
Alaska				X	X		X		X			X		
Arizona			X	X	X	X	X	X	X	X	X	X	X	
Arkansas				X	X		X	X			X	X	X	
California			X	X	X	X	X	X	X	X	X	X		
Colorado				X	X	X		X	X					
Connecticut					X		X		X					
Delaware				X	X	X			X		X	X		
District of Columbia		X	X	X	X	X	X	X	X	X	X	X		
Florida				X	X	X			X		X			There is no state-mandated norm-referenced testing. However, the state collects information furnished by local districts that elect to perform norm-referenced testing. The FCAT is administered to Grades 4, 8, and 10 to assess reading and Grades 5, 8, and 10 to assess math.
Georgia	X			X	X	X	X		X			X		
Hawaii				X			X		X		X			The Credit by Examination is voluntary and is given in Grade 8 in Algebra and Foreign Languages.
Idaho				X	X	X	X	X	X	X	X	X		
Illinois				X	X	X		X	X		X	X		Exit Exam failure will not disqualify students from graduation if all other requirements are met.
Indiana				X			X		X		X			
Iowa		*	*	*	*	*	*	*	*	*	*	*	*	*Iowa does not currently have a statewide testing program. Locally chosen assessments are administered to grades determined locally.
Kansas				X	X	X		X	X		X	X		

STATE	KG	1	2	3	4	5	6	7	8	9	10	11	12	COMMENT
Kentucky					X	X	X	X	X	X	X	X	X	
Louisiana				X	X	X	X	X	X	X	X	X	X	
Maine					X				X			X		
Maryland				X		X			X	X	X	X	X	
Massachusetts				X	X	X		X	X	X	X			
Michigan					X	X		X	X					
Minnesota				X		X			X	X	X	X	X	
Mississippi				X	X	X	X	X	X					Mississippi officials would not return phone calls or emails regarding this information.
Missouri			X	X	X	X	X	X	X	X	X			
Montana					X				X			X		The State Board of Education has decided to use a single norm-referenced test statewide beginning 2000–2001 school year.
Nebraska		**	**	**	**	**	**	**	**	**	**	**	**	**Decisions regarding testing are left to the individual school districts.
Nevada					X				X					Districts choose whether and how to test with norm-referenced tests.
New Hampshire				X			X				X			
New Jersey				X	X			X	X	X	X	X		
New Mexico					X		X		X					
New York				X	X	X	X	X	X	X			X	Assessment program is going through major revisions.
North Carolina	X			X	X	X	X		X	X			X	NRT Testing selects samples of students, not all.
North Dakota					X		X		X		X			
Ohio					X		X			X			X	
Oklahoma				X		X		X	X			X		
Oregon				X		X			X		X			

STATE	KG	1	2	3	4	5	6	7	8	9	10	11	12	COMMENT
Pennsylvania						X	X		X	X		X		
Rhode Island				X	X	X		X	X	X	X	X		
South Carolina				X	X	X	X	X	X	X	X	***	***	***Students who fail the High School Exit Exam have opportunities to take the exam again in grades 11 and 12.
South Dakota			X		X	X			X	X		X		
Tennessee			X	X	X	X	X	X	X					
Texas				X	X	X	X	X	X		X	X	X	
Utah		X	X	X	X	X	X	X	X	X	X	X	X	
Vermont					X	X	X		X	X	X	X		Rated by the Centers for Fair and Open Testing as a nearly model system for assessment.
Virginia				X	X	X	X		X	X		X		
Washington					X			X			X			
West Virginia				X	X	X	X	X	X	X	X	X		
Wisconsin					X				X		X			
Wyoming					X				X			X		

Testing Accommodations

The more testing procedures vary from one classroom or school to the next, the less we can compare the scores from one group to another. Consider a test in which the publisher recommends that three sections of the test be given in one 45-minute session per day on three consecutive days. School A follows those directions. To save time, School B gives all three sections of the test in one session lasting slightly more than two hours. We can't say that both schools followed the same testing procedures. Remember that the test publishers provide testing procedures so schools can administer the tests in as close a manner as possible to the way the tests were administered to the groups used to obtain test norms. When we compare students' scores to norms, we want to compare apples to apples, not apples to oranges.

Most schools justifiably resist making any changes in testing procedures. Informally, a teacher can make minor changes that don't alter the testing procedures, such as separating two students who talk with each other instead of paying attention to the test; letting Lisa, who is getting over an ear infection, sit closer to the front so she can hear better; or moving Jeffrey away from the window to prevent his looking out the window and daydreaming.

There are two groups of students who require more formal testing accommodations. One group of students is identified as having a disability under Section 504 of the Rehabilitation Act of 1973 (Public Law 93-112). These students face some challenge but, with reasonable and appropriate accommodation, can take advantage of the same educational opportunities as other students. That is, they have a condition that requires some accommodation for them.

Just as schools must remove physical barriers to accommodate students with disabilities, they must make appropriate accommodations to remove other types of barriers to students' access to education. Marie is profoundly deaf, even with strong hearing aids. She does well in school with the aid of an interpreter, who signs her teacher's instructions to her and tells her teacher what Marie says in reply. An appropriate accommodation for Marie would be to provide the interpreter to sign test instructions to her, or to allow her to watch a videotape with an interpreter signing test instructions. Such a reasonable accommodation would not deviate from standard testing procedures and, in fact, would ensure that Marie received the same instructions as the other students.

If your child is considered disabled and has what is generally called a Section 504 Plan or individual accommodation plan (IAP), then the appropriate way to ask for testing accommodations is to ask for them in a meeting to discuss school accommodations under the plan. If your child is not already covered by such a plan, he or she won't qualify for one merely because you request testing accommodations.

The other group of students who may receive formal testing accommodations are those identified as handicapped under the Individuals with Disabilities Education Act (IDEA)—students with mental retardation, learning disabilities, serious emotional disturbance, orthopedic handicap, hearing or visual problems, and other handicaps defined in the law. These students have been identified under procedures governed by federal and sometimes state law, and their education is governed by a document called the Individualized Educational Program (IEP). Unless you are under a court order specifically revoking your educational rights on behalf of your child, you are a full member of the IEP team even if you and your child's other parent are divorced and the other parent has custody. Until recently, IEP teams actually had the prerogative to exclude certain handicapped students from taking standardized group testing altogether. However, today states make it more difficult to exclude students from testing.

If your child is classified as handicapped and has an IEP, the appropriate place to ask for testing accommodations is in an IEP team meeting. In fact, federal regulations require IEP teams to address testing accommodations. You have the right to call a meeting at any time. In that meeting, you will have the opportunity to present your case for the accommodations you believe are necessary. Be prepared for the other team members to resist making extreme accommodations unless you can present a very strong case. If your child is identified as handicapped and you believe that he or she should be provided special testing accommodations, contact the person at your child's school who is responsible for convening IEP meetings and request a meeting to discuss testing accommodations.

Problems arise when a request is made for accommodations that cause major departures from standard testing procedures. For example, Lynn has an identified learning disability in mathematics calculation and attends resource classes for math. Her disability is so severe that her IEP calls for her to use a calculator when performing all math problems. She fully under-

stands math concepts, but she simply can't perform the calculations without the aid of a calculator. Now it's time for Lynn to take the school-based standardized tests, and she asks to use a calculator. In this case, since her IEP already requires her to be provided with a calculator when performing math calculations, she may be allowed a calculator during school standardized tests. However, because using a calculator constitutes a major violation of standard testing procedures, her score on all sections in which she is allowed to use a calculator will be recorded as a failure, and her results in some states will be removed from among those of other students in her school in calculating school results.

How do we determine whether a student is allowed formal accommodations in standardized school testing and what these accommodations may be? First, if your child is not already identified as either handicapped or disabled, having the child classified in either group solely to receive testing accommodations will be considered a violation of the laws governing both classifications. Second, even if your child is already classified in either group, your state's department of public instruction will provide strict guidelines for the testing accommodations schools may make. Third, even if your child is classified in either group and you are proposing testing accommodations allowed under state testing guidelines, any accommodations must still be both *reasonable* and *appropriate*. To be reasonable and appropriate, testing accommodations must relate to your child's disability and must be similar to those already in place in his or her daily educational program. If your child is always tested individually in a separate room for all tests in all subjects, then a similar practice in taking school-based standardized tests may be appropriate. But if your child has a learning disability only in mathematics calculation, requesting that all test questions be read to him or her is inappropriate because that accommodation does not relate to his identified handicap.

Glossary

Accountability   The idea that a school district is held responsible for the achievement of its students. The term may also be applied to holding students responsible for a certain level of achievement in order to be promoted or to graduate.

Achievement test   An assessment that measures current knowledge in one or more of the areas taught in most schools, such as reading, math, and language arts.

Aptitude test   An assessment designed to predict a student's potential for learning knowledge or skills.

Content validity   The extent to which a test represents the content it is designed to cover.

Criterion-referenced test   A test that rates how thoroughly a student has mastered a specific skill or area of knowledge. Typically, a criterion-referenced test is subjective, and relies on someone to observe and rate student work; it doesn't allow for easy comparisons of achievement among students. Performance assessments are criterion-referenced tests. The opposite of a criterion-referenced test is a norm-referenced test.

Frequency distribution   A tabulation of individual scores (or groups of scores) that shows the number of persons who obtained each score.

Generalizability   The idea that the score on a test reflects what a child knows about a subject, or how well he performs the skills the test is supposed to be assessing. Generalizability requires that enough test items are administered to truly assess a student's achievement.

Grade equivalent   A score on a scale developed to indicate the school grade (usually measured in months of a year) that corresponds to an average chronological age, mental age, test score, or other characteristic. A grade equivalent of 6.4 is interpreted as a score that is average for a group in the fourth month of Grade 6.

High-stakes assessment   A type of standardized test that has major consequences for a student or school (such as whether a child graduates from high school or gets admitted to college).

Mean   Average score of a group of scores.

Median   The middle score in a set of scores ranked from smallest to largest.

National percentile   Percentile score derived from the performance of a group of individuals across the nation.

Normative sample   A comparison group consisting of individuals who have taken a test under standard conditions.

Norm-referenced test A standardized test that can compare scores of students in one school with a reference group (usually other students in the same grade and age, called the "norm group"). Norm-referenced tests compare the achievement of one student or the students of a school, school district, or state with the norm score.

Norms A summary of the performance of a group of individuals on which a test was standardized.

Percentile An incorrect form of the word *centile,* which is the percent of a group of scores that falls below a given score. Although the correct term is *centile,* much of the testing literature has adopted the term *percentile.*

Performance standards A level of performance on a test set by education experts.

Quartiles Points that divide the frequency distribution of scores into equal fourths.

Regression to the mean The tendency of scores in a group of scores to vary in the direction of the mean. For example: If a child has an abnormally low score on a test, she is likely to make a higher score (that is, one closer to the mean) the next time she takes the test.

Reliability The consistency with which a test measures some trait or characteristic. A measure can be reliable without being valid, but it can't be valid without being reliable.

Standard deviation A statistical measure used to describe the extent to which scores vary in a group of scores. Approximately 68 percent of scores in a group are expected to be in a range from one standard deviation below the mean to one standard deviation above the mean.

Standardized test A test that contains well-defined questions of proven validity and that produces reliable scores. Such tests are commonly paper-and-pencil exams containing multiple-choice items, true or false questions, matching exercises, or short fill-in-the-blanks items. These tests may also include performance assessment items (such as a writing sample), but assessment items cannot be completed quickly or scored reliably.

Test anxiety Anxiety that occurs in test-taking situations. Test anxiety can seriously impair individuals' ability to obtain accurate scores on a test.

Validity The extent to which a test measures the trait or characteristic it is designed to measure. Also see *reliability.*

Answer Keys for Practice Skills

Chapter 2:
Addition

1 C
2 B
3 C
4 C
5 B
6 A
7 A
8 A

Chapter 3:
Subtraction

1 D
2 A
3 B
4 D
5 B
6 A
7 A
8 B

Chapter 4:
Multiplication

1 B
2 A

3 D
4 C
5 B
6 A
7 C
8 A
9 C
10 C
11 A
12 C
13 C
14 B
15 B
16 C
17 A
18 B

Chapter 5:
Division

1 B
2 C
3 C
4 D
5 C
6 A

Chapter 6:
Fractions and
Probability

1 B
2 C
3 A
4 A
5 B
6 D
7 C
8 B
9 A
10 B

Chapter 7:
Decimals

1 C
2 C
3 B
4 A
5 B
6 A
7 D
8 C
9 A
10 C

Chapter 8:
Standard and Metric
Measurements

1 C
2 A
3 C
4 D
5 B
6 C
7 B
8 A
9 B
10 C

Chapter 9:
Geometry

1 A
2 C
3 B
4 A
5 D
6 A
7 C
8 A
9 C
10 C

Sample Practice Test

You may be riding a roller coaster of feelings and opinions at this point. If your child has gone through the preceding chapters easily, then you're both probably excited to move on, to jump in with both feet, take the test, and that will be that. On the other hand, your child may have struggled a bit with some of the chapters. Some of the concepts may be difficult for him and will require a little more practice. Never fear!

All children acquire skills in all areas of learning when they are developmentally ready. We can't push them, but we can reinforce the skills that they already know. In addition, we can play games and do activities to pave the way for their understanding of the skills that they will need to master later. With luck, that's what you've done with the preceding chapters.

The test that follows is designed to incorporate components of several different kinds of standardized tests. The test that your child takes in school probably won't look just like this one, but it should be sufficiently similar that he should be pretty comfortable with the format. The administration of tests varies as well. It is important that your child hear the rhythm and language used in standardized tests. If you wish, you may have your child read the directions that precede each test section to you first and explain what the item is asking him to do. Your child may try it on his own if you feel he understands it, or you may want to clarify the instructions.

Test Administration

If you like, you may complete the entire test in one day, but it is not recommended that your child attempt to finish it in one sitting. As test administrator, you'll find that you'll need to stretch, have a snack, or use the bathroom too! If you plan to do the test in one day, leave at least 15 minutes between sessions.

Before you start, prepare a quiet place, free of distractions. Have two or three sharpened pencils with erasers that don't smudge and a flat, clear work space. As your child proceeds from item to item, encourage him to ask you if he doesn't understand something. In a real testing situation, questions are accepted, but the extent to which items can be explained is limited. Don't go overboard in making sure your child understands what to do. Your child will have to learn to trust his instincts somewhat.

The test shouldn't take all day. If your youngster seems to be dawdling along, enforce time limits and help him to understand that the real test will have time limits as well. Relax, and try to have fun!

To the Student:

These tests will give you a chance to put the tips you have learned to work.
   A few last reminders . . .

- Be sure you understand all the directions before you begin each test. You may ask the teacher questions about the directions if you do not understand them.

- Work as quickly as you can during each test.

- When you change an answer, be sure to erase your first mark completely.

- You can guess at an answer or skip difficult items and go back to them later.

- Use the tips you have learned whenever you can.

- It is OK to be a little nervous. You may even do better.

   Now that you have completed the lessons in this book, you are on your way to scoring high!

Addition

1 (A)(B)(C)(D)	3 (A)(B)(C)(D)	5 (A)(B)(C)(D)	7 (A)(B)(C)(D)	9 (A)(B)(C)(D)	11 (A)(B)(C)(D)
2 (A)(B)(C)(D)	4 (A)(B)(C)(D)	6 (A)(B)(C)(D)	8 (A)(B)(C)(D)	10 (A)(B)(C)(D)	12 (A)(B)(C)(D)

Subtraction

1 (A)(B)(C)(D)	3 (A)(B)(C)(D)	5 (A)(B)(C)(D)	7 (A)(B)(C)(D)	9 (A)(B)(C)(D)	11 (A)(B)(C)(D)
2 (A)(B)(C)(D)	4 (A)(B)(C)(D)	6 (A)(B)(C)(D)	8 (A)(B)(C)(D)	10 (A)(B)(C)(D)	

Multiplication

1 (A)(B)(C)(D)	4 (A)(B)(C)(D)	7 (A)(B)(C)(D)	10 (A)(B)(C)(D)	13 (A)(B)(C)(D)	16 (A)(B)(C)(D)
2 (A)(B)(C)(D)	5 (A)(B)(C)(D)	8 (A)(B)(C)(D)	11 (A)(B)(C)(D)	14 (A)(B)(C)(D)	17 (A)(B)(C)(D)
3 (A)(B)(C)(D)	6 (A)(B)(C)(D)	9 (A)(B)(C)(D)	12 (A)(B)(C)(D)	15 (A)(B)(C)(D)	18 (A)(B)(C)(D)

Division

1 (A)(B)(C)(D)	3 (A)(B)(C)(D)	5 (A)(B)(C)(D)	7 (A)(B)(C)(D)	9 (A)(B)(C)(D)	11 (A)(B)(C)(D)
2 (A)(B)(C)(D)	4 (A)(B)(C)(D)	6 (A)(B)(C)(D)	8 (A)(B)(C)(D)	10 (A)(B)(C)(D)	

Fractions and Probability

1 (A)(B)(C)(D)	3 (A)(B)(C)(D)	5 (A)(B)(C)(D)	7 (A)(B)(C)(D)	9 (A)(B)(C)(D)	11 (A)(B)(C)(D)
2 (A)(B)(C)(D)	4 (A)(B)(C)(D)	6 (A)(B)(C)(D)	8 (A)(B)(C)(D)	10 (A)(B)(C)(D)	

Decimals

1 (A)(B)(C)(D)	3 (A)(B)(C)(D)	5 (A)(B)(C)(D)	7 (A)(B)(C)(D)	9 (A)(B)(C)(D)	11 (A)(B)(C)(D)
2 (A)(B)(C)(D)	4 (A)(B)(C)(D)	6 (A)(B)(C)(D)	8 (A)(B)(C)(D)	10 (A)(B)(C)(D)	

Measurement

1 (A)(B)(C)(D)	4 (A)(B)(C)(D)	6 (A)(B)(C)	8 (A)(B)(C)(D)	10 (A)(B)(C)	12 (A)(B)(C)
2 (A)(B)(C)(D)	5 (A)(B)(C)(D)	7 (A)(B)(C)	9 (A)(B)(C)(D)	11 (A)(B)(C)	13 (A)(B)(C)(D)
3 (A)(B)(C)(D)					

Geometry

1 (A)(B)(C)(D)	4 (A)(B)(C)(D)	6 (A)(B)(C)(D)	8 (A)(B)(C)(D)	10 (A)(B)(C)(D)	12 (A)(B)(C)(D)
2 (A)(B)(C)(D)	5 (A)(B)(C)(D)	7 (A)(B)(C)(D)	9 (A)(B)(C)(D)	11 (A)(B)(C)(D)	13 (A)(B)(C)(D)
3 (A)(B)(C)(D)					

ADDITION

Directions: Solve each problem below.

Example:

What is the estimated answer for 61 + 32?

A 93

B 90

C 95

D 50

Answer:

A 90

1 What is the estimated answer for 254 + 443? (Round to nearest hundred.)

A 400 + 600 = 1,000

B 300 + 500 = 800

C 300 + 400 = 700

D none of the above

2 What is the estimated answer for 228 + 542? (Round to nearest hundred.)

A 520 + 740 = 1,260

B 200 + 500 = 700

C 600 + 700 = 1,300

D none of the above

3 What is the estimated answer for 48 + 87?

A 50 + 90 = 140

B 40 + 90 = 130

C 40 + 80 = 120

D none of the above

4 What is the estimated answer for 2,923 + 5,328? (Round to nearest thousand.)

A 2,000 + 5,000 = 7,000

B 1,000 + 4,000 = 5,000

C 3,000 + 5,000 = 8,000

D none of the above

5 Solve (2 + 3) + 5 = ___.

A 1 + 5 = 6

B 6 + 5 = 11

C 5 + 5 = 10

D none of the above

6 Solve (4 + 9) + 7 = ___.

A 5 + 7 = 12

B 13 + 7 = 20

C 13 + 7 = 10

D none of the above

GO

7 Solve $(10 + 12) + 10 =$ ___.

    A $22 + 10 = 31$

    B $2 + 10 = 12$

    C $22 + 10 = 32$

    D   none of the above

8 Cindy drove with her family from New York to California to see her grandparents. They drove 420 miles on Monday, 680 miles on Tuesday, and 565 miles on Wednesday. Calculate both the estimation of the miles traveled and the actual miles traveled.

    A   estimation is 1,800 and actual is 1,765

    B   estimation is 1,700 and actual is 1,665

    C   estimation is 1,600 and actual is 1,605

    D   none of the above

9 At the candy store, a 1-pound box of chocolates costs $4.49 and an 8-ounce box costs $2.29. If Tom buys one of the larger boxes and two of the smaller boxes, what was the total cost?

    A $4.49 + $4.49 + $2.29 = $11.18

    B $4.49 + $2.29 + $2.29 = about $8.00

    C $4.49 + $2.29 + $2.29 = $9.07

    D   none of the above

10 Jill helps her mother by keeping track of her family's food purchases for a month. Their weekly grocery bills were $65.22, $62.99, $48.24, and $84.72. Her mother also stopped several times a week at the local market to buy milk, which costs $1.89 a gallon. If the family used 6 gallons of milk for the month, what was their monthly milk bill? How much did they pay for milk and groceries?

    A $11.34 for milk, $272.51 for milk and groceries

    B $11.34 for milk, $262.51 for milk and groceries

    C $4.11 for milk, $262.23 for milk and groceries

    D   none of the above

11 The food store offers a 1-pound T-bone steak on sale for $4.99 a pound. If Sam buys 2 pounds of T-bone steak instead of a package of hamburger for $6.89, how much will the steak cost?

    A $6.89

    B $9.98

    C   4.99

    D   none of the above

12 Carlos and Susan are trying to buy the cheapest container of mayonnaise. The store is selling a half-pint serving at $1.29, a pint serving at $2.49, two quarts for $4.78, and a gallon at $11.56. Which is the most economical way to buy mayonnaise?

    A   half pints at $1.29

    B   pints at $2.49

    C   2 quarts for $4.78

    D   a gallon at $11.56

STOP

SUBTRACTION

Directions: Solve each problem below.

Example: What is the estimated answer for 522 – 399? (Round to nearest hundred.)

    A   500 – 300

    B   500 – 400

    C   525 – 400

    D   400 – 300

Answer:

    B   500 – 400

---

1 What is the estimated answer for 489 – 168? (Round to nearest hundred.)

    A   500 – 200 = 300

    B   400 – 200 = 200

    C   400 – 100 = 300

    D   none of the above

---

2 What is the estimated answer for 423 – 298? (Round to nearest hundred.)

    A   500 – 400 = 100

    B   400 – 300 = 100

    C   500 – 298 = 202

    D   none of the above

---

3 Kenu's family traveled 432 miles on Monday and 305 miles on Tuesday. How much farther did the family travel on Monday than on Tuesday?

    A   543 – 345 = 198

    B   345 – 543 = 202

    C   500 – 300 = 200

    D   none of the above

---

4 At the candy store, an 8-ounce box of chocolates costs $5.49, and a 4-ounce box costs $3.29. If Jane needs 8 ounces and she wants to save the most money, should she buy the larger box or two smaller boxes?

    A   She should buy the large box for $5.49.

    B   She should purchase two smaller boxes for $3.29 each.

    C   The costs would be the same, so it doesn't matter.

    D   None of the above

---

5 George bought a shirt for $31.99 and a pair of socks for $2.29. If he gave the clerk two $20 bills, how much change did he receive?

    A $36.28

    B $5.72

    C $3.43

    D   none of the above

GO

6 Ari's father bought $10.59 worth of gas on Monday, and $11.54 worth of gas the next week. How much more did he spend for gas the second week?

A $0.85

B $0.95

C $1.95

D none of the above

7 Mrs. Ming bought a car on credit that cost $8,756. She paid $1,020 right away. How much does she still owe on the car?

A $7,345

B $7,636

C $7,020

D none of the above

8 Hank is a quarterback who threw 176 passes. Only 123 were caught. How many weren't caught?

A 54

B 53

C 123

D none of the above

9 6,523
− 332

A 6,191

B 6,291

C 6,855

D none of the above

10 4,007
− 996

A 5,003

B 3,011

C 4,011

D none of the above

11 1,394
− 452

A 942

B 1,942

C 1,946

D none of the above

STOP

MULTIPLICATION

Directions: Solve each problem below.

Example: $(2 \times 1) + (2 \times 0) =$ ___

   A   2

   B   0

   C   6

   D   4

Answer:

   A   2

---

1 $(3 \times 3) + (2 \times 3) =$ ___

   A $6 + 5 = 11$

   B $9 + 18 = 27$

   C $9 + 6 = 15$

   D   none of the above

---

2 $(9 \times 8) - (3 \times 2) =$ ___

   A $17 - 1 = 16$

   B $72 - 6 = 66$

   C $72 + 9 = 81$

   D   none of the above

---

3 $(8 \times 4) - 3 =$ ___

   A $32 - 3 = 29$

   B $12 - 6 = 6$

   C $40 - 3 = 37$

   D   none of the above

---

4 Which equation has the largest product, $(8 \times 7) - (3 \times 8)$ or $(7 \times 8) + (3 \times 0)$?

   A $(8 \times 7) - (3 \times 8)$ because the difference is 75

   B $(7 \times 8) + (3 \times 0)$ because the sum is 56

   C $(7 \times 7) + (3 \times 0)$ because the sum is 72, and that is more than the product of 55

   D   none of the above

---

5 Julio is having a party at school with 20 friends. He wants to have 2 balloons for each friend at the party and 1 party hat for each. How many balloons and how many hats must he buy?

   A   20 balloons and 40 hats

   B   40 balloons and 20 hats

   C   20 balloons and 20 hats

   D   none of the above

---

6 Juanita likes to play Jeopardy with her two friends. If she wants to award two prizes to each of her two friends, and she plans to play six rounds, how many prizes will Julia need for her two friends in all?

   A   She will need 12 prizes.

   B   She will need 23 prizes.

   C   She will need 3 prizes.

   D   none of the above

GO

MATH, GRADE FOUR: GET READY!

7 Ben and his father are installing an invisible fence to keep their dog on their square lawn. They will need 2 lengths of wire for each side of the yard. How many lengths of wire must Ben and his father prepare?

A $2 + 4 = 6$

B $2 \times 4 = 8$

C $2 \times 6 = 12$

D none of the above

8 Bill and his mother are buying cupcakes for a class picnic. If there are 12 children at school and they want to buy 3 cupcakes for each child, how many total cupcakes must Bill and his mother buy?

A $3 \times 12 = 48$

B $12 + 3 = 15$

C $3 \times 12 = 36$

D none of the above

Directions: Multiply.

Example:

$2,000 \times 6 = $ ___

A 120,000

B 12,000

C 2,000

D 6,000

Answer:

B 12,000

9 $2,000 \times 5 = $ ___

A 2,000

B 7,000

C 10,000

D 0,000

10 $70 \times 80 = $ ___

A 9,000

B 5,000

C 5,600

D 56,000

11 $300 \times 40 = $ ___

A 12,000

B 1,200

C 7,000

D 70,000

12 $600 \times 50 = $ ___

A 50,000

B 60,500

C 30,000

D 300,000

13 $20 \times 80 = $ ___

A 800

B 16,000

C 4,000

D 1,600

14 $900 \times 5 = $ ___

A 45,000

B 4,500

C 200,000

D 5,400

GO

Directions: Multiply and find the correct answer.

Example:

    38
    ×32

    A   1,216

    B   160

    C   2,984

    D   2,216

Answer:

    A   1,216

---

15   39
        ×34

    A   1,206

    B   1,247

    C   1,188

    D   1,326

16   25
        ×43

    A   559

    B   1,075

    C   602

    D   1,076

---

17   63
        ×74

    A   1,012

    B   4,662

    C   968

    D   989

---

18   31
        ×23

    A   713

    B   723

    C   263

    D   293

STOP

DIVISION

Directions: Complete each problem.

Example:

$525 \div 5 =$ ___

A   105

B   5

C   25

D   20

Answer:

A   105

---

1 $536 \div 4 =$ ___

A   135

B   179, r 3

C   134

D   not given

---

2 $36 \div 6 =$ ___

A   6

B   7

C   5

D   not given

---

3 $40 \div$ ___ $= 10$

A   5

B   4

C   2

D   not given

---

4 $72 \div$ ___ $= 9$

A   8

B   6

C   2

D   5

Directions: Read the following problems and choose the correct answer. Remember to calculate the quotient inside the parentheses before adding or subtracting another number.

Example:

$(12 \div 2) + 2 =$ ___

A   6

B   8

C   12

D   1

Answer:

B   8

---

5 $(10 \div 2) + 5 =$ ___

A   10

B   5

C   15

D   none of the above

---

6 $(4 \div 2) + 2 =$ ___

A   5

B   6

C   12

D   none of the above

GO

7 $(12 \div 3) + 9 =$ ___

   A   5

   B   45

   C   13

   D   none of the above

8 $(36 \div 6) - 2 =$ ___

   A   4

   B   34

   C   8

   D   none of the above

9 $2\overline{)12}$

   A   3

   B   4

   C   6

   D   none of the above

10 $4\overline{)20}$

   A   3

   B   4

   C   5

   D   none of the above

11 $8\overline{)75}$

   A   9

   B   9, r 2

   C   9, r 3

   D   none of the above

STOP

FRACTIONS AND PROBABILITY

Directions: Solve each problem below.

Example:

$$\frac{1}{5} + \frac{2}{5} = \underline{}$$

A $\frac{2}{5}$

B $\frac{3}{5}$

C $\frac{4}{5}$

D $\frac{0}{5}$

Answer:

B $\frac{3}{5}$

---

1 $\frac{7}{10} + \frac{2}{10} = \underline{}$

A $\frac{9}{20}$

B $\frac{9}{10}$

C 29

D none of the above

---

2 $\frac{1}{4} + \frac{2}{4} = \underline{}$

A $\frac{1}{4}$

B $\frac{3}{4}$

C $\frac{4}{4}$

D none of the above

---

3 $\frac{11}{12} - \frac{3}{12} = \underline{}$

A $\frac{8}{24}$

B $\frac{14}{12}$

C $\frac{8}{12}$

D none of the above

---

4 Find $\frac{3}{5}$ of 10.

A 4

B 6

C 5

D none of the above

---

5 Multiply to find two equivalent fractions for ⅓.

A ²/₄ and ³/₆

B ¼ and ⁴/₆

C ³/₉ and ⁴/₁₂

D none of the above

---

6 Divide to find two equivalent fractions for ⁶/₁₂.

A ½ and ²/₄

B ⅓ and ²/₆

C ²/₁₀ and ⁴/₃

D none of the above

GO

7 Write this fraction in simplest form: $^8/_{16}$

  A $^6/_9$

  B $^4/_{16}$

  C $^1/_3$

  D none of the above

8 Choose the improper fraction.

  A $^1/_2$

  B $^3/_4$

  C $^6/_3$

  D none of the above

9 Rename this improper fraction as a mixed number *in its simplest form:* $^{18}/_5$

  A $2^2/_5$

  B $3^3/_5$

  C $3^1/_3$

  D none of the above

10 Rename this improper fraction as a mixed number *in its simplest form:* $^{18}/_4$

  A $4^2/_4$

  B $4^1/_2$

  C $3^1/_2$

  D none of the above

11 A die has 6 sides numbered from 1 to 6. If you roll the die one time, what is the chance of getting a 6?

  A $^3/_6$

  B $^1/_6$

  C $^2/_6$

  D none of the above

STOP

DECIMALS

Directions: Solve each problem below.

Example:

In the number 521.47, what digit is in the *tenths* place?

A 0

B 5

C 4

D 2

Answer:

C 4

---

1 For the number 357.3, what digit is in the *tenths* place?

A 4

B 3

C 7

D 6

---

2 Write this number in standard form: three hundred twenty-two and thirty-three hundredths.

A 322.033

B 302.03

C 322.33

D none of the above

---

3 Order these decimals from largest to smallest: 5.8, 4.9, 8.1, 8.3.

A 8.3, 8.1, 5.8, 4.9

B 8.1, 8.3, 5.8, 4.9

C 4.9, 5.8, 8.1, 8.3

D none of the above

---

4 Use either >, <, or = to compare these two decimals: 3.2 ___ 3.20.

A 3.2 < 3.20

B 3.2 = 3.20

C 3.2 > 3.20

D none of the above

---

5 Write the decimal numbers for these fractions: $\frac{30}{100}$, $\frac{3}{10}$, $\frac{3}{100}$.

A .30 .3 .003

B .30 .03 .003

C .30 .3 .03

D none of the above

Cut along dashed line.

GO

6 Write the fraction and the decimal for the shaded area in the figure below.

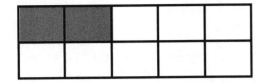

   A   ²/₁₀ or .2

   B   ²/₁₀₀ or .02

   C   ²/₁₀ or .02

   D   none of the above

7 Write the fraction and the decimal for the shaded area in the figure below.

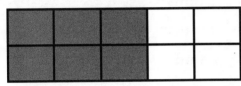

   A   ⁴/₁₀ or .4

   B   ⁶/₁₀ or .06

   C   ⁶/₁₀ or .6

   D   ⁴/₁₀ or .04

8 Add $23.05 and $19.75.

   A $42.68

   B $32.068

   C $42.80

   D   none of the above

9 Convert to decimals and add: $5\frac{8}{10} + 4\frac{1}{10}$.

   A   5.10 + 4.2 = 10.30

   B   4.70 + 4.02 = 10.72

   C   9.7 + 4.2 = 10.9

   D   none of the above

10 You bought a sled at a yard sale for $5.34. You gave the cashier a ten dollar bill. How much change will you receive?

   A $4.46

   B $4.00

   C $4.56

   D $4.66

11 Solve the problem: 249.2 + 38.76 = ___.

   A   about 300

   B   287.96

   C   397.06

   D   none of the above

STOP

MEASUREMENT

Directions: Solve each problem below.

Example:

How many inches are in 3 feet?

A 24

B 36

C 12

D 20

Answer:

B 36

---

1 How many inches are in 4 feet?

A 48 inches

B 18 inches

C 24 inches

D none of the above

---

2 How many feet are in 3 yards?

A 3

B 6

C 9

D none of the above

---

3 How many inches are equivalent to 2 yards?

A 98 inches

B 72 inches

C 36 inches

D none of the above

---

4 How many feet are equal to 4 yards?

A 3 feet

B 48 feet

C 12 feet

D none of the above

---

5 How many yards are equivalent to 72 inches?

A 2 yards

B 4 yards

C 3 yards

D none of the above

---

6 Which is longer, 10 centimeters or 2 meters?

A 2 meters

B 10 centimeters

C They are equal.

---

7 Which is heavier, 2 pounds or 32 ounces?

A 2 pounds

B 32 ounces

C They are equal.

---

8 How would you measure a book?

A in inches

B in yards

C in feet

D in miles

9 What is the best way to measure your bedroom?

    A   inches

    B   cups

    C   miles

    D   feet

10 Which is more, 3 cups or 1 quart?

    A   3 cups

    B   1 quart

    C   They are equal.

11 Which is more, 4 quarts or 1 gallon?

    A   4 quarts

    B   1 gallon

    C   They are equal.

12 Which is less, 1,000 grams or 1 kilogram?

    A   1,000 grams

    B   1 kilogram

    C   They are equal.

13 What is the best container to fill a bathtub with water the fastest?

    A   a measuring cup

    B   a gallon jug

    C   a teaspoon

    D   a pint jar

STOP

GEOMETRY

Directions: Read each question and choose the correct answer.

Example:

Choose the cube.

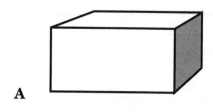

A

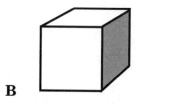

B

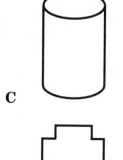

C

D

Answer:

B

1   A can of soup is shaped most like a what?

    A   cube

    B   cylinder

    C   rectangular prism

    D   sphere

2   Which of the following shapes is a triangle?

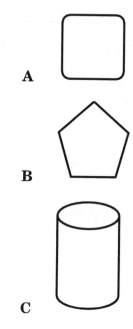

A

B

C

D

GO

3 Which of these shapes is a square?

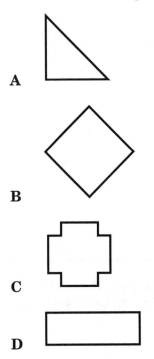

A

B

C

D

4 What is the area of this shape? (Area = length × width.)

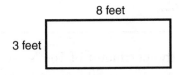

8 feet

3 feet

A 36 feet

B 12 feet

C 24 feet

D 48 feet

5 What is the area of this shape?

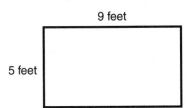

9 feet

5 feet

A 45 feet   B 40 feet

C 28 feet   D 9 feet

6 What angles are in the figure below?

A right angles

B acute angles

C obtuse angles

D no angles

7 Which of these is an octagon?

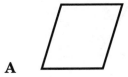

A

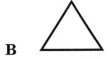

B

C

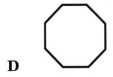

D

GO

8 How many faces does the figure below have?

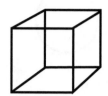

A 5

B 8

C 4

D 6

9 What angles are in the figure below?

A right angles

B obtuse angles

C acute angles

D no angles

10 The figure below is called a what?

A ray

B parallel line

C line

D line segment

11 The lines below are what?

A parallel

B perpendicular

C slanted

D intersecting

12 What is the area of your living room if two sides are each 8 feet and two sides are each 12 feet?

A 12 feet

B 24 feet

C 32 feet

D 96 feet

13 What is the perimeter of Tom's rectangular skating rink if it is 60 feet long and 50 feet wide?

A 200 feet

B 220 feet

C 2,200 feet

D 22 feet

Cut along dashed line.

STOP

Answer Key for Sample Practice Test

Addition

1 C
2 B
3 A
4 C
5 C
6 B
7 C
8 B
9 C
10 A
11 B
12 C

Subtraction

1 A
2 B
3 D
4 A
5 B
6 B
7 D
8 B
9 A
10 B
11 A

Multiplication

1 C
2 B
3 A
4 B
5 B
6 D
7 B
8 C
9 C
10 C
11 A
12 C
13 D
14 B
15 D
16 B
17 B
18 A

Division

1 C
2 A
3 B
4 A
5 A
6 D
7 C
8 A
9 C
10 C
11 C

Fractions and Probability

1 B
2 B
3 C
4 B
5 C
6 A
7 D
8 C
9 B
10 B
11 B

Decimals

1 B
2 C
3 A
4 B
5 C
6 A
7 C
8 C
9 D
10 D
11 B

Measurement

1 A
2 C
3 B
4 C
5 A
6 A
7 C
8 A
9 D
10 B
11 C
12 C
13 B

Geometry

1 B
2 D
3 B
4 C
5 A
6 D
7 D
8 D
9 C
10 C
11 D
12 D
13 B

JV